The First Commandment

Be Fruitful, and Multiply

William H. Noah

www.avalonpress.net

ISBN

0-9724708-0-8 $12.00

Dedicated to my bride, Melody,
and the fruit of her womb:
Mary Lu, Margaret, and Meredith

CONTENTS

FOREWORD

If you are looking for a book that helps you argue against some social illness; one that builds your faith through relating some heroic experiences; one that through guilt tries to motivate you to greater Christian service; one that shares a recipe for fixing some failing relationship; or even one that confirms a biblical principal in a new or novel way: you've got the wrong book.

If you are like me, you have read one or more books in the aforementioned categories and you came away inspired; but then you returned to a state of spiritual dryness too quickly. And if you are like me, in your innermost being, the part of you that you rarely (if ever) share with anyone, you have wondered if you really are in relationship with Jesus Christ. Good news: if you are willing to sacrifice anything, even your most treasured assumptions, to build an intimate, relevant relationship with your Lord, then this book might help.

Working on this book helped open my eyes to some fundamental flaws in my spiritual understanding. Shoring up my biblical foundation has allowed me to start building a relationship with my Creator as it has never been before. Not that this book has some magical formula or that everyone who reads this book will come away changed. But the truths that God has shared with Bill (Dr. Noah) might just free you to grow your relationship with your Savior into the kind that you always knew was possible.

Ray Fitzgerald

INTRODUCTION

Have you ever considered why you are here? If you believe in a Creator, then why did He fashion you the way you are? Why did He create us with distinct personalities, different preferences, as well as strong emotions and will? The Bible tells us God created us for one principal reason: to have a relationship with Him. "God created man in his own image" (Gen. 1:27) because He desired communion (fellowship) with him: "All things were created by him, and for him" (Col. 1:16). The whole meaning of life and our purpose for existence is to have an intimate relationship with the Creator (Isa. 43; 1 Cor 1:9).

But throughout history, man has mostly rejected this closeness with God. We acknowledge His position and authority, but we often desire relationships with other men and women instead of with the Creator Himself. In the garden Adam chose to follow Eve in disobedience instead of following God (Gen. 3:6–7), and the Israelites chose to listen to Moses rather than God at Mount Sinai (Ex. 20:19). And so it continued through history.

Yet God still pursued a relationship with human beings. Out of eternal love God became a man Himself, Jesus of Nazareth (John 1:1,14). Yet men rejected Him as well: "He came unto his own, and his own received him not" (John 1:11). Christ came to His own people, to those who claimed to be His children, and they rejected Him (Matt. 23:37). Even today, many who call themselves God's children reject

Christ by spending time with other believers instead of with Christ Himself. The purpose of creation is that we should know God intimately, and Jesus defined this knowledge as "life eternal, that they might know thee the only true God, and Jesus Christ, whom thou hast sent" (John 17:3). Jesus came to earth proclaiming a relationship with God, but because of His audience's widespread rejection, Jesus said, "Narrow is the way, which leadeth unto [eternal] life, and few there be that find it" (Matt. 7:14).

God's design for this relationship with us is grounded in the earliest recorded words He spoke to man: "Be fruitful, and multiply" (Gen. 1:28). These words were also God's first commandment to man. Many believe God's first commandment was Deuteronomy 6:5—"Thou shalt love the LORD thy God with all thine heart, with all thy soul, and with all thy might"—or Exodus 20:3—"Thou shalt have no other gods before me." Some may even suggest Genesis 2:17: "Of the tree of the knowledge of good and evil, thou shall not eat of it." None of these was actually first.

Jesus referred to the Deuteronomy passage in Mark 12:29–30, suggesting it may have been first in importance, but it wasn't in chronology. Exodus 20:3 was the first of the Ten Commandments Moses received at Mount Sinai, but by this time much had already happened in human history— God had interacted with Noah, Abraham, and countless other individuals and obviously had given man many commandments already—so this was not the initial order either.

And Genesis 2:17, while a commandment, followed Genesis 1:28 in its appearance. No, of all the endlessly possible things that our Creator could have said to His new creation, He chose "Be fruitful, and multiply." And He did so because, as we shall see, in this mandate is our purpose.

After knowing God for many years and being involved in much ministry work and evangelism, I became aware of a shallowness of my relationship to Him. Worse yet, I realized that I, as well as many others, was trapped in this shallowness because of incorrect understanding. As I began to separate myself from the many entanglements of this life and spend more and more time with my Creator, I began to see the purpose within this first commandment.

In this book I will share with you the many layers of meaning I discovered in a study of God's first commandment to mankind. Together we will explore how throughout God's Word He has expressed His desire for a closer relationship with each one of us, as well as how we opt for other relationships instead. We will learn how to maintain a purposeful connection to Jesus, the source of all life. We will examine the benefits of "pruning" sin from one's life, the snares of religiosity, and the other half of the gospel: the fact that we must die with Jesus. And through all of this, we will come to understand more fully how to obey God's first commandment: "Be fruitful, and multiply."

Understanding and knowledge by themselves produce only pride, for "knowledge puffeth up, but charity edifieth" (1 Cor. 8:1).

I write this not in hope that you will simply increase in knowledge, but rather that you will deepen your relationship with God. True, many have little interest in knowing their Creator, but for those few who honestly desire to walk the "narrow road" of closeness with God, I give this book to you.

We should travel this road of discovery as the Bereans of Acts 17:11, who were open to any new teaching but searched the Scriptures daily to see if the teaching was true. Guided by the Holy Spirit (John 16:13), we will lay one stone of truth upon another, or rather "precept upon precept; line upon line" (Isa. 28:10) as we build a more intimate connection with God. The foundation's name is Jesus Christ.

This book does not contain any new rules or doctrines to follow, but rather revelation from God's Spirit with biblical reference to encourage those willing few toward more meaningful fellowship with their Creator. This is why He created us and what "eternal life" means: to know Him.

The first precept is the first commandment, "Be fruitful, and multiply."

Chapter 1
Be Fruitful . . .

"So God created man in his own image, in the image of God created he him; male and female created he them. And God blessed them, and God said unto them, Be fruitful and multiply" (Gen. 1:27–28). These four English words, "be fruitful and multiply," represent only two words in the original Hebrew: *parah*, meaning "make fruitful or bear fruit" and *rabah*, meaning "multiply or make abundant." "*Parah rabah*" or "be fruitful and multiply" was such an important concept to God, He chose to deliver it to man before all of His other commands.

Noah received the same commandment from God after the Flood. God had destroyed the whole surface of the earth and all mankind except for Noah and his family. When he and his kin came off the ark, "God blessed Noah and his sons, and said unto them, Be fruitful, and multiply, and replenish the earth" (Gen. 9:1).

God also referred to this commandment in Genesis 17, when He changed His servant Abram's name to Abraham and promised to "multiply thee exceedingly" and "make thee exceeding fruitful, and I will make nations of thee" (vv. 2,6). This implied that Abraham was to be fruitful and multiply. In this particular instance, God actually gave this commandment as a promise.

Next to hear these words was Abraham's grandson Jacob. Another name change took place in Genesis 35, when God gave Jacob the name Israel. "And God said unto him, I am God Almighty, be fruitful and multiply; a nation and a company of nations shall be of thee, and kings shall come out of thy loins" (Gen. 35:11).

Later God gave this first commandment through Moses to the descendants of Jacob (the Israelites): "For I will have respect unto you, and make you fruitful, and multiply you, and establish my covenant with you" (Lev. 26:9). God desired the Israelites to "be fruitful and multiply," but they would not obey. So in the fullness of time, God brought forth John the Baptist, who again touched on this commandment, saying, "Bring forth therefore fruits worthy of repentance" (Luke 3:8).

In the New Testament, the Lord Jesus taught this first commandment several times. A well-known passage is John 15:1–2: "I am the true vine, and my Father is the husbandman. Every branch in me that beareth not fruit he taketh away: and every branch that beareth fruit [be fruitful] he purgeth it, that it may bring forth more fruit [multiply]." Jesus commanded that we should bear fruit, and from that, we should bring forth more fruit, which is multiplying.

Later in the same passage, Jesus said, "Herein is my Father glorified, that ye bear much fruit; so shall ye be my disciples" (John 15:8). We glorify our Father in heaven by bearing fruit and fulfilling the first commandment. In fact, God designed us to do so. Jesus said, "Ye have not chosen me, but I have chosen you, and ordained you, that ye should go and bring forth fruit, and that your fruit should remain" (John 15:16).

In addition to the Gospels, the letters of Paul teach the first commandment. In Philippians 4:17 he wrote, "I desire fruit [be fruitful] that may abound [multiply] to your account." Paul also wrote to the Colossians of "the gospel . . . which . . . bringeth forth fruit" (1:5–6). God tells us through Paul to bear fruit.

What Is Fruit?

As we recognize that God's first commandment was indeed to "be fruitful, and multiply," immediately a question arises: what is "fruit"? Many understand this commandment as pertaining to having children. True, when God told Adam, Noah, Abraham, Jacob, and the children of Israel to "be fruitful and multiply," he was referring, at least in part, to reproduction. Children are "the fruit of the womb" (Ps. 127:3), and it is through having children that we multiply. But that is not the purpose of this writing.

Paul told us that the experiences of Adam, Noah, Abraham, Jacob, and the Israelites are illustrations God uses to reveal truth to us today (1 Cor. 10:6,11). When Jesus and Paul instructed us to bear fruit, I do not believe they were referring to "the fruit of the womb" but rather to spiritual fruit in the kingdom of God. "God is a Spirit: and they that worship him must worship him in spirit and truth" (John 4:24). And it is from this "spiritual fruit" that we multiply the kingdom of God. So what is the fruit, or should I say, what does the fruit represent?

Paul answered this when he referred to "the fruit of the Spirit." Galatians 5:22–23 says, "The fruit of the Spirit is love, joy, peace, longsuffering [patience], gentleness, goodness, faith, meekness [humility], temperance [self-control]." This is the spiritual fruit that God desires to harvest. These are the fruits that God desired Adam, Noah, Abraham, and Jacob and his descendants to produce, and the ones Jesus commands us today to produce.

Known by Our Fruits

The relationship between a husband and wife produces "the fruit of the womb," and these children usually look and behave like their parents. They are a reflection of their parents, and the parents are often known by their fruit or children. It is

4

the same in the kingdom of God; the relationship between the Lord Jesus, the Husband (Rom. 7:4), and a Christian, the bride, produces the fruit of the Spirit. The fruit is a reflection of Christ, and it is the evidence of God's Spirit within us.

Not only are we to bear this fruit, *but this fruit also identifies us as God's*. In Matthew 12:33 Jesus said, "Either make the tree good, and his fruit good; or else make the tree corrupt, and his fruit corrupt; for the tree is known by his fruit." Only those who are born of God will produce good fruit. It is what separates and marks the child of God. Many trees look very similar, but their fruit is what distinguishes one tree from another, and it is the same with people.

In Matthew 7:16–20 Jesus expounded on this idea more fully:

> Ye shall know them by their fruits. Do men
> gather grapes of thorns, or figs of thistles? Even
> so every good tree bringeth forth good fruit; but
> a corrupt tree bringeth forth evil fruit. A good
> tree cannot bring forth evil fruit, neither can a
> corrupt tree bring forth good fruit. Every tree
> that bringeth not forth good fruit is hewn down,
> and cast into the fire. Wherefore by their fruits
> ye shall know them.

Jesus was saying that the presence of these fruits reveals the presence of the Holy Spirit in another person. Only the Spirit of God can produce this fruit; our flesh cannot.

In contrast to the good fruit, which is the evidence of God's Spirit, the corrupt, evil, or poison fruit is the evidence of our flesh. Galatians 5:17 says, "For the flesh lusteth against the Spirit, and the Spirit against the flesh: and these are contrary the one to the other." Paul then listed what God considers bad fruit: adultery, fornication, idolatry, hatred, wrath, heresies, murders, drunkenness (vv. 19–21). These and others like them are the poisoned fruits of our flesh that God commands us to avoid.

God the Farmer

This contrast in fruit is the focus of the two parables of vineyards in Scripture. First, the prophet Isaiah pictured Israel as a vineyard. In chapter 5, verse 4, God asked, "What could have been done more to my vineyard that I have not done in it? Wherefore, when I looked that it should bring forth grapes, brought it forth wild [poison] grapes." Even though God had done everything possible to make this vineyard perfect and fruitful, it brought forth bad fruit instead of good. In fact, in verse 10 we see: "Yea, ten acres of vineyard shall yield one bath [approximately five to ten gallons]." Can you imagine ten acres of grapevines producing only a few gallons of wine? God judged the vineyard in verse 6: "And I will lay it waste: it shall not be pruned, nor digged; but there shall come up briers and thorns: I will also command the clouds that they rain no rain upon it."

God wanted Israel to produce His fruit, but instead they produced their own—and it was poison. Just as God judged the vineyard, He also judged Israel: "Therefore my people are gone into captivity, because they have no knowledge: and their honourable men are famished, and their multitude dried up with thirst" (v. 13). The Israelites did not understand, with all of their knowledge, how to produce good fruit; we should take heed.

Jesus told the second parable of a vineyard in Matthew 21:33–41. Here God was a "householder" (or landowner) who sent his slaves (the prophets) and then finally his son (Jesus) to the husbandmen (Jews) to collect their fruit. In response, the Jews beat and killed all of His messengers. Because the Israelites produced only bad fruits such as hatred, envy, greed, wrath, and murder, they, too, would face God's judgment, Jesus said.

How Many Fruits Are There?

As you know, fruits come in more than two varieties—good or bad. Galatians 5 lists nine different spiritual fruits. Are there others? Does the Scripture suggest more qualities that will identify us as God's?

The apostle John's description of heaven, or more specifically the holy city, includes a tree of life "which bare twelve manner of fruits" (Rev. 22:2). The tree of life, which also appeared in the Garden of Eden, certainly produced only spiritual fruit, or the fruit of the Spirit.

7

Twelve is an important number in biblical history. The nation of Israel began as twelve fruits (of the womb) or sons of Jacob. In heaven, or the new Jerusalem, the twelve gates in the city wall represent the twelve sons, for on those gates the names of the twelve tribes of the sons of Israel are inscribed (Rev. 21:12). In addition, the wall of the city has twelve foundation stones and inscribed on them are the names of the twelve apostles of the Lamb (Rev. 21:14). So you see, it's no accident that the tree of life bears twelve different fruits; these are the fruit of the Spirit.

Proverbs 11:30 seems to confirm this: "The fruit of the righteous is a tree of life." This verse does not necessarily say that righteousness is a fruit (although it may be), but rather that the righteous produce fruit, and that this fruit is a "tree of life." God commanded the righteous in the beginning to produce fruit; therefore the fruit on this tree of life is the fruit of the Spirit. And the tree of life in Revelation bears twelve distinct fruits.

What Are the Other Three?

Now the first nine fruits, as we've seen, are quite obvious from Galatians 5. But what are the other three? Ephesians 5:9 says, "The fruit of the Spirit is in all goodness and righteousness and truth." Paul mentioned three possible fruits here: goodness, righteousness, and truth. Goodness is already among the nine fruits of Galatians 5; therefore, we need consider only righteousness and truth.

First, let's look at righteousness as a fruit. Second Timothy 2:22 says, "Flee also youthful lusts: but follow righteousness, faith, charity, peace, with them that call on the Lord out of a pure heart." In this verse, Paul listed righteousness with three known fruits of the Spirit, suggesting that it is an individual fruit itself. In James 3:18, the Lord's brother wrote, "The fruit of righteousness is sown in peace of them that make peace." These two passages by themselves make a good case for righteousness being one of the twelve fruits on the tree of life.

Ephesians 5:9 suggests that truth is also a fruit of the Spirit. Just as Scripture tells us to "walk in the Spirit" (Gal. 5:25), it also commends those who "walk in truth" (2 John 4; 3 John 3–4). The apostle John also referred to the "Spirit of truth" (John 14:17, 15:26, 16:13; 1 John 4:6). In fact, 1 John 5:6 says, "The Spirit is truth," and Jesus actually described Himself as "the truth" (John 14:6). Certainly, those who possess God's Spirit will manifest and love the truth.

If righteousness and truth are the tenth and eleventh fruits, then what is the twelfth? There are several possibilities, but the two most likely are mercy and hope. A number of verses strongly suggest mercy as being a fruit of the Spirit. Micah 6:8 is a good example: "He hath shewed thee, O man, what is good: and what doth the LORD require of thee, but to do justly, and to love mercy, and to walk humbly with thy God?" All of such verses (Matt. 5:7; Gal. 6:16; 1 Tim. 1:2; 2 Tim. 1:2; Titus 1:4; 2 John 3; Jude 2) list mercy with other known fruits of the Spirit. Notice in James 3:17–18 that the author included mercy on a list with the fruits of peace, gentleness, and righteousness.

As far as hope being the twelfth fruit, the strongest evidence is 1 Corinthians 13:13, which says, "And now abideth faith, hope, charity, these three; but the greatest of these is charity." Here Paul grouped hope with the fruits of love and faith. Biblical authors listed hope with faith in 1 Peter 1:21 and with the fruit of joy in 1 Thessalonians 2:19.

Whether or not hope is a fruit of the Spirit, I am unsure. Whether or not mercy is a fruit, I still have some questions. *But these things we know for certain: there are at least nine fruits of the Spirit, and God commands us to exhibit all of them as part of His first commandment to "Be fruitful, and multiply."*

What the Fruit Is Not

Although being fruitful refers to bearing the fruit of the Spirit, many teach that the fruit represents good works. This is a common misunderstanding. Good works often result from fruit, but they are not fruit themselves. Paul wrote, "Walk worthy of the LORD unto all pleasing, being fruitful in every good work, and increasing in the knowledge of God" (Col. 1:10). Paul instructed us to be fruitful or productive in our works, implying a difference between them. He did not say "being fruitful by our works," which would equate good works with fruit. No, we are to bear fruit in whatever we do; therefore, the fruit is not "doing" or works.

Our Lord Jesus made this point clear in speaking of the false prophets who did "wonderful works" but did not produce good fruit:

> Beware of false prophets, which come to you in sheep's clothing, but inwardly they are ravening wolves. Ye shall know them by their fruits . . . Every tree that bringeth not forth good fruit is hewn down, and cast into the fire. Wherefore by their fruits ye shall know them. Not every one that saith unto me, Lord, Lord, shall enter into the kingdom of heaven; but he that doeth the will of my Father which is in heaven. Many will say to me in that day, Lord, Lord, have we not prophesied in thy name? And in thy name have cast out devils? And in thy name done many wonderful works? And then will I profess unto them, I never knew you: depart from me.
> (Matt. 7:15–16, 19–23)

These false prophets did marvelous deeds but displayed no fruit of the Spirit. These good works made them appear outwardly like innocent sheep, but inwardly they were still wicked wolves. In other words, their behavior was the same as that of the true children of God, but their hearts were still evil. If we look for fruit, we will not be deceived.

11

Furthermore, they did all these works in the name of Jesus, and these wolves actually called themselves Christians. But Jesus warned us: "Take heed that no man deceive you. For many shall come in my name, saying, I am Christ; and shall deceive many" (Matt. 24:4–5). I used to think that this passage was suggesting that many would come claiming to be Christ themselves, but that is not so. Jesus was speaking here in the first person. If He were referring to others claiming to be Christ, He would have said, "For many will come in my name, saying, [they are] Christ." No, the deceivers (wolves) will come saying that Jesus is the Christ, the Anointed, the Son of God. Yet they will cause many to err.

We must remember that throughout 1,950 years of church history, deceivers proclaiming that Jesus is the Messiah and calling themselves Christian have hated, verbally assaulted, imprisoned, tortured, and even killed millions of true Christians. In fact, many of these wolves in sheep's attire are deceived themselves; they believe they are sheep and that they are actually serving God by enforcing their views, excommunicating, and in times past, even imprisoning and killing those who disagree with them.

Today, many unfortunate souls continue to follow deceivers who claim Jesus is the Messiah, the Son of God. These deceivers may preach or sing about Jesus but lead many into bondage. You might know someone who has a tremendous voice or great musical talent, and when he sings a hymn or spiritual song you receive a great blessing, but that is a work and not fruit. You may know someone who is a powerful preacher or orator, and you enjoy his sermons, or you may know someone who can perform miraculous signs and wonders, but these all are just works. These works are not necessarily evidence of a child of God; only the fruit is evidence. Jesus never said we will know them by their message or talent, but by their fruit.

These statements are difficult to hear, but Paul warned: "For I know this, that after my departing shall grievous wolves enter in among you, not sparing the flock . . . to draw away disciples after them" (Acts 20:29–30). Remember, these wolves look like sheep; they are not hanging out in sleazy places. They are mingling among us in churches and ministries. They are not outside the body of Christ but within it. And they are leaders (v. 30). This incorrect teaching of works being fruit allows the wolves to go unnoticed, but if we focus on fruit, we would not be fooled. We must become fruit-oriented and not works-oriented.

It is also important to mention that fruit is not souls won through evangelism. Though this concept is commonly taught, it is not scriptural. At the end of time, when the Lord takes up His harvest, He will be looking for fruit, not souls. A harvest is always for fruit, not souls. In Mark 4:29, Jesus referred to this action: "When the fruit is brought forth, immediately he putteth in the sickle, because the harvest is come." John also records Jesus describing the harvester as one who "gathereth fruit unto life eternal" (4:36). And in Luke our Lord asked, "When the Son of man cometh, shall he find faith [a fruit] on the earth?" (18:8)

No, fruit does not symbolize men's souls or their works. It is the evidence of God's Spirit within us and represents love, joy, peace, patience, and so on. I believe there are twelve in all, as Revelation's tree of life reveals. God commanded Adam, Noah, Abraham, Jacob, and the Israelites to bear this fruit, and He expects the same from us today. Even "though [we] speak with tongues of men and angels, and have not [the fruit of love, we are] become as sounding brass, or a tinkling cymbal" (1 Cor. 13:1). This fruit is how we are known, and how we know others. This keeps us from deceiving ourselves as well as being deceived by others, and this is why it is God's first commandment.

Chapter 2
. . . And Multiply

Although fruit does not represent souls, the first commandment does contain God's instruction to win souls. The
increase in number resulting from souls won is multiplying,
which is the second part of the first commandment. Again,
winning souls is multiplying, not bearing fruit. God's commandment implies "Be fruitful, and [then] multiply."
Evangelism means "good message," but it's not necessarily the
good message that multiplies the kingdom of God—it is
"good fruit." And in the kingdom of God, fruit is required
before multiplication can occur.

Fruit must precede multiplication in God's creation as well.
Multiplication occurs from the seeds, and the seeds are either
in the fruit or are the fruit. In the case of an apple, the seed is
in the fruit. In the case of wheat, the seed is the fruit. "And
God said, Let the earth bring forth . . . the fruit tree yielding
fruit after his kind, whose seed is in itself" (Gen. 1:11). If you

do not have any fruit, you cannot have any seed, and therefore, you cannot multiply.

Just as seeds are inside fruits such as apples, olives, or watermelons, seeds are also inside the "fruit of the womb." Whether it is a lamb, a calf, or a child, each contains seed from which it can multiply. This multiplying may result in a flock, a herd, or even grandchildren. Producing children or "the fruit of the womb" is merely increasing in number, not multiplying. But if my three children utilize the seed within them to have three children each, then I am multiplying (3x3=9).

In the same way that the reproductive seed lies inside a grape or a man, the spiritual seed to multiply the kingdom of God lies inside our spiritual fruit: "love, joy, peace, longsuffering, gentleness, goodness, faith, meekness, temperance," righteousness, truth, mercy, or hope. This is a hard saying for some, but people receive the kingdom of God through our love, joy, humility, and other spiritual fruit, not our message. Multiplying or winning souls comes from the seed of the Spirit contained within the fruit of the Spirit, and *we spread the kingdom of God via our fruit, not our knowledge or experience.* Without fruit, we cannot multiply, and our words are just empty, religious phrases.

Jesus Is the Seed

In the spiritual kingdom of God, our primary command is to produce spiritual fruit containing spiritual seed to multiply.

This is pure, untainted, everlasting seed. Peter wrote that we are "being born again, not of corruptible seed, but of incorruptible, by the word of God, which liveth and abideth for ever" (1 Peter 1:23). This verse says that we are born again "by the word of God," implying that the "incorruptible seed" is the "word." In fact, Luke 8:11 plainly says, "The seed is the word of God." This is the "incorruptible seed" of 1 Peter 1:23 and 1 Corinthians 15:36–54. It is the same seed in the parable of the sower and the remainder of Scripture.

But the seed is not the Scripture itself; it is Jesus. These statements are not referring to the written word or Bible. The Greek term for *word* in both these verses is *logos* and represents the unpolluted spiritual seed from which we are born again. John explained who this seed was in his gospel: "In the beginning was the Word [*logos*], and the Word [*logos*] was with God, and the Word [*logos*] was God . . . And the Word [*logos*] was made flesh, and dwelt among us, (and we beheld his glory, the glory as of the only begotten of the Father,) full of grace and truth" (John 1:1,14). Who became flesh and dwelt among us? Not the Bible, but Jesus, and He is the "only begotten of the Father." Jesus is the *logos* or Word of God, and thus Jesus is the Seed.

He is the seed inside the fruit on the tree of life, and therefore, the seed inside our love, joy, peace, patience, goodness, kindness, faith, humility, self-control, and so on. Once we receive Jesus, then we can fulfill the first commandment and "be fruitful, and multiply" in the kingdom of God.

God plants the seed of the tree of life in us when we receive Jesus and begin a relationship with Him. God took the tree of life from man after the Fall (Gen. 3:23–24), but Jesus' death and burial replanted this tree to bring forth much fruit (John 12:24). As we grow spiritually, the tree of life in us bears the fruit of the Spirit, which has seeds to multiply.

As the seeds come forth from the fruit, there are many ways they are scattered. One way is the wind, and it is interesting that the English words *wind* and *spirit* in the New Testament are from the same Greek word *pneuma*. In John 3:8 Jesus said that the wind, representing the Spirit, blows wherever it desires; as it blows, it carries seed. Therefore the Holy Spirit (wind) blows the seed from our fruit wherever He desires and plants this seed in hearts of those He chooses. Though it is God who gives "the increase" (1 Cor. 3:7), we play a part. Just as in nature most of the seeds fall next to the tree, the seeds we plant mainly land in those who are close to us in relationship. God instructs us to plant this seed in others by His Spirit. Paul "planted" as an example for us (1Cor. 3:6)

Where Seeds Grow Best

This concept of Jesus being the Seed is evident in His parables. The parable of the sower is the first in the New Testament and possibly the most important, as Jesus affirmed when He asked, "Know ye not this parable? And how then will ye know all parables?" (Mark 4:13) This parable appears in three of the Gospels (Matt. 3:3–23; Mark 4:2–20; Luke 8:4–15), and its whole purpose is to teach us how to obey the first commandment.

As we seek to understand the parable, we need to recognize what the soil represents. Mark 4:15 states that the seed was "sown in their hearts." Since we sow seed in soil, soil must represent the heart of man. The parable of the sower speaks of four different types of soil, or hearts: that "by the way side," the "stony ground," the earth "among thorns," and the "good ground" (Mark 4:4–8). The most obvious difference in the soils is that only the fourth type produced fruit.

The first, the soil "by the wayside," never even germinated the seed. The second, the "stony ground," sprouted, but it withered before it produced mature fruit. The third, that "among thorns," was choked by the weeds and "yielded no fruit" (v. 7). What were the weeds, specifically? Mark 4:19 says, "The cares of this world, and the deceitfulness of riches, and the lusts of other things." Only the fourth soil or heart bore fruit. Only the good ground, which represents a good heart, fulfilled the first commandment.

Not only did this fourth soil, the good ground (heart), produce fruit, it produced great yields: "Some thirty, some sixty, and some an hundred" times increase (Mark 4:8). This is multiplying.

In the same way, *the spiritual Seed, Jesus, received in the right heart will produce much fruit of the Spirit.* From this vast increase in spiritual fruit, there is a tremendous availability of "incorruptible" seed, which God's Spirit plants in others through us. Second Corinthians 9:10 says, "Multiply your seed sown, and increase the fruits of your righteousness." We multiply seed by first producing fruit, and God can then harvest this fruit to collect more seed to sow. As we receive Jesus into our hearts, the tree of life begins to grow in us, and God again says, *"Parah rabah."*

Beware Worldly Multiplying

Because our hearts, not our message, contain God's Seed, if our message alone causes us to multiply, then we may be propagating only the kingdoms of this world. Insightful Bible preaching, inspiring music, and a nurturing atmosphere will not multiply the kingdom of God. We must first have fruit. We can reproduce the kingdoms or organizations of this world through charisma, entertainment, talent, witchcraft, manipulation, guilt, and all the deeds of the flesh (poison fruits), but we cannot expand the kingdom of God by such means.

Worldly organizations today, as through history, try to multiply in order to appear fruitful. This is not God's way; this is the world's: searching for numbers and not God. In fact, many equate numbers with success and God's blessing, but God never says that they will know us by our multiplication or numbers. He says, "Ye shall know them by their fruits" (Matt. 7:16). We must not focus on multiplication, but rather focus first on fruit.

Unfortunately, many churches and ministries operate with this mentality. Remember, Jesus said that numerous fake Christians would come in His name claiming that He is the true Messiah, but they will deceive many (Matt. 24:5). The deception is using the name and teachings of Jesus to build an organization and following. These wolves in sheep's clothing focus on the message, doctrine, and numbers instead of fruit. There are even many true Christians who are unknowingly building worldly kingdoms in the name of Jesus because of incorrect understanding, and others are merely following just a "message" because they don't know to look for fruit.

We must repent of our worldly ways. It is not how many can hear our message, but rather how many can taste our joy, unconditional love, patience, and other spiritual fruit. As they taste our fruit they will receive the Seed inside the fruit, Jesus. Otherwise, it is just men following men, and not men being actually born of God, and we are failing to fulfill the second half of God's first command, "Be fruitful, and multiply."

Chapter 3
Fruit Through Relationship

As we receive the Seed for the kingdom of God, we begin a relationship—or covenant—with Jesus Christ. God gives the first commandment, "Be fruitful, and multiply," only to those who are in covenant with Him, and *it is only through relationship that we bear fruit.* When God spoke the first commandment to Noah, Abraham, Jacob, and the children of Israel through Moses, He made a covenant with each of them at the same time (Gen. 9:7–9, 17:2–6, 35:11; Lev. 26:9). Comparatively, God had created Adam in relationship or covenant with Himself, and therefore He had no need to establish one before He delivered the first commandment.

What does *covenant* mean? Today, we often employ the words *contract* or *vow* (oath or promise) instead. Partners in business will use a contract to define their relationship. Sometimes a community will have restrictive covenants that define or determine the relationship (what is allowed) between the individuals who live there. In addition, a bride and groom often exchange vows in a ceremony in an attempt to define their relationship as they enter the covenant of marriage.

The original Greek word translated "covenant" is *diatheke*, and it represents specifically the relationship between God and man. The Latin word is translated "testament," and this is where we get the names of the Old Testament and New Testament. These two parts of the Bible would actually be better titled the Old Relationship (Old Covenant) with God, and the New Relationship (New Covenant) with God.

This type of relationship often has a mediator between the parties involved, and today this person is usually a lawyer. The old relationship (*diatheke* or testament) had a mediator; his name was Moses. The new relationship has a Mediator as well. His name is Jesus, and it is through Him that we now have relationship with God.

Vine and Branches

One of the images the Bible gives us of this relationship is that of a plant. Jesus said, "I am the true vine, and my Father is the husbandman [farmer]" (John 15:1), and we are the branches. The farmer plants the vine, and as branches, we relate to the farmer through the vine. The farmer can supply nutrients to the branches only via the vine. The branches receive life only from the their mediator, the vine. We receive life only from our Mediator, the Lord Jesus, "for there is one

God, and one mediator between God and men, the man Christ Jesus" (1 Tim. 2:5).

This relationship of the branch to the vine is necessary for the branch to bear fruit, just as our relationship to Jesus is required for us to bear fruit. Jesus said, "I am the vine, ye are the branches: he that abideth in me, and I in him, the same bringeth forth much fruit: for without me ye can do nothing" (John 15:5). *As branches, we must be connected to the true Vine, Jesus, to fulfill the first commandment and produce the fruit of the Spirit.*

Bridegroom and Bride

Another of the images the Bible gives us of our relationship with God is that of marriage. In this case, the wife (us) is to abide in the husband (Jesus) in order to yield fruit. "Ye should be married to another, even to him who is raised from the dead, that we should bring forth fruit unto God" (Rom. 7:4). "For I am jealous over you with godly jealousy: for I have espoused you to one husband, that I may present you as a chaste virgin to Christ" (2 Cor. 11:2; see also Eph. 5:22–23; Rev. 19:7–9). We the bride are married to Jesus the Bridegroom so that we may bear fruit to the Father. Christ is the Husband, and those who receive His seed are His bride. Just as a husband places his seed in his bride to produce "the fruit of the womb," Christ places His seed in us to yield the fruit of the Spirit.

24

We see these images again and again throughout Scripture. Remember that children are the fruit of marriage: "Lo, children are an heritage of the LORD: and the fruit of the womb is his reward" (Ps. 127:3). As the husband places seed in the wife, she "abides" in her husband through intimacy, and fruit is produced in the womb as children. In fact, Psalm 128:3 says, "Thy wife shall be as a fruitful vine [producing children] by the sides of thine house." Through the relationship (covenant) of marriage, the wife is to produce fruit (children).

Bear or Burn

A branch is useful only if it bears fruit, and every branch that does not bear fruit is broken off. "If a man abide not in me, he is cast forth as a branch, and is withered; and men gather them, and cast them into the fire, and they are burned" (John 15:6). In fact, as we read in a previous chapter, "Every tree that bringeth not forth good fruit is hewn down, and cast into the fire" (Matt. 7:19). Today, those of us who are married to—in covenant with—the Lord Jesus are to produce the fruit of Spirit. Anyone who claims to be married to Jesus, yet does not produce the fruit of the Spirit, will receive His anger or wrath, especially at the Last Judgment (consider the judgment of the sheep and goats—Matt. 25:31–46).

Men sometimes complain that their children do not follow, and that their wives do not abide. What can you do?

Younger children can be disciplined in the fruit of love, but you cannot make older children or wives follow. Their wills are at work. But you can love them as Christ loved the church (Eph. 5:25) and respond with the fruit of patience as God is patient with you in your rebellion. We must not react with poison fruit such as anger. It is possible that God may be using your wife's lack of intimacy to show you your lack of intimacy with your Husband, Christ. Maybe your child's rebellion serves to demonstrate your own disobedience to your Father in heaven. As branches, we will never be treated worse than men treated the "true vine" (Jesus). Just as you want your wife to be intimate with you, Christ wants you to spend private time with Him. It is the purpose of creation.

Fruit is a reflection of the tree, for a good tree will yield only good fruit. In the same way, a corrupt tree will produce evil or poison fruit. As I get older, my physical appearance resembles more and more that of my earthly father and people even say they see my father in me. This thought forces some tough questions: When others see our lives, do they see our heavenly Father as evidenced by His fruit? Do they see "love, joy, peace, longsuffering, gentleness, goodness, faith, meekness, temperance"? Or do they see the poison fruits of the flesh? Would Jesus tell us what He told the Pharisees: "Ye are of your father the devil, and the lusts [poison fruits] of your father ye will do" (John 8:44)?

In John 15:6, Jesus told us basically to bear fruit or burn. This is a strong teaching from our Lord, and we should again take heed. Note that a fruit tree *exists*; it does not *do*. It is a life of being and not doing. We must draw all we have from Him as the branch draws from the vine. We bear fruit only in relationship with God. A branch cannot draw from another branch; it must draw from the vine (Jesus). We must do the same.

Faith Is a Fruit

We must know someone before we can trust him. Trust or faith comes through experience, and experience with someone is a relationship. As we have seen, we can produce fruit only through a relationship with God, and faith is a fruit of the Spirit.

Although the scope of this writing does not include the individual characteristics of the twelve different fruits of the Spirit, I should address one particular fruit here and now: faith. It is translated from the Greek word *pistis* and occurs more than six hundred times in the New Testament. When *pistis* occurs as a verb, it is translated as "believe," and when *pistis* occurs as a noun, it is translated as "faith." *Pistis* and its derivatives all have the same meaning: trust. Having faith is to believe, but to believe with confidence enough to trust.

It is a trust that goes beyond circumstances or what our eyes can see. "Now faith is the substance of things hoped for, the evidence of things not seen" (Heb. 11:1). We are to "walk by faith, not by sight" (2 Cor. 5:7). Faith is seeing "the invisible things of him [God]" (Rom. 1:20). Faith is not trusting in the worldly circumstances we see with our eyes; rather it is relying upon the Lord. Solomon wrote, "Trust in the LORD with all thine heart; and lean not unto thine own understanding" (Prov. 3:5). When we lean on something, we are trusting in it. We must trust God, not our understanding.

Since faith is a fruit, we know it comes from God and not from our own devices. "God hath dealt to every man the measure of faith" (Rom. 12:3), and we receive this initial "measure" when He calls us and we hear His words. The more we hear Him, the more we can trust Him because faith comes from experience, good or bad. My wife's faith in me comes from more than twenty years of experience with me, not from some vow I made to her at the altar. Her faith is based on our relationship: hearing my words and seeing my actions. Even more, trust in a marriage is dependent on the private relationship, not how she or I appear in public.

In the same way, faith (trust) in Jesus also comes through experience, not by a promise or vow. Many today are trusting in a commitment they have made at the altar to Jesus, and yet they have no real relationship with Him. These have little faith. Without a relationship, they can't hear Him (Rom. 10:17), and their faith cannot increase. As in marriage, our faith in Christ is only as strong as the relationship we have with Him in private; it does not necessarily reflect how we appear before men. Therefore, if we find we have little faith, it is because we have little relationship with the God who gives it.

Childlike Faith

The Scripture pictures us not only as branches and as a bride, but as God's children. "For as many as are led by the Spirit of God, they are the sons of God" (Rom. 8:14). "Beloved, now are we the sons of God" (1 John 3:2).

This should be a particularly welcoming image to us. God clearly carries much affection and regard for children. Jesus said, "Suffer [allow] the little children to come unto me, and forbid them not: for of such is the kingdom of God. Verily I say unto you, Whosoever shall not receive the kingdom of God as a little child, he shall not enter therein" (Mark 10:14–15). In this chapter of Mark, Jesus rebuked His disciples for keeping young ones from Him. He said that the kingdom of God is for little children, and in order to find entrance to it, we must receive it the way a little child would.

This may seem odd, but think about it: small children have tremendous trust in their parents, for that is all they know. There is nothing else in which they can put their trust. Children "lean not unto [their] own understanding" because they do not have much understanding. Unlike older children and adults, small children concern themselves only with where their parents are, for their parents provide for all their needs and security.

When well disciplined, small children are such a joy. And it is their trust or faith in us that makes them so delightful. This is the faith that Enoch had that "pleased God. But without faith it is impossible to please him: for he that cometh to

God must believe [have faith] that he is [exists]" (Heb. 11:5–6). It is childlike faith that gives God pleasure. God desires us to come to Him as little children, sit on His lap, and call Him "Abba" ("Daddy" in Aramaic) (Mark 14:36; Rom. 8:15; Gal. 4:6). We are to yield the fruit of faith, and God has chosen a small child to be our example (Matt. 18:4).

In contrast, many older children in our culture have little faith or trust in their parents. As children grow, they develop their own understanding and begin to trust in it, and as they develop relationships outside their immediate family, they can begin to trust in those as well. Sure, they will continue to take for granted the food, clothing, housing, money, and time their parents provide, and they may even admit they have parents, but they often do not trust in them.

So it often is with our Father in heaven. We may claim to be children of God, yet we mainly trust in ourselves and our "own understanding." Sure, we call on God in desperation when all our efforts fail, just like the teenagers who call on their parents only when their friends cannot help; we also take for granted all the provisions that God has given us, just as many teenagers do. This is because our relationship with God is so shallow, and our faith is so weak. *We should have the faith of a small child, not a teenager.*

I should point out here that the problem with many older children is often their own parents. As parents, did we provide the proper seed? The Seed (Jesus) for the kingdom of God is in the fruit of the Spirit, not in lectures or anger. Children may through proper training become very moral, successful adults, but they cannot have God's fruit unless we have planted His seed in them. For our children to receive the spiritual Seed from us, we must first produce fruit ourselves. As parents, we must first examine our own lives before those of our children.

Faith is a fruit, and we have already seen that fruit is dependent on a relationship or covenant. These two, covenant and faith, are eternally linked. As we pursue a relationship with God, our faith in Him will mature. As we seek stronger ties and relations to this world, we will trust more in the things of this world, and have less faith in God.

A life of faith is a holy life. God said, "Ye shall be holy; for I am holy" (Lev. 11:44). Being holy literally means being set apart from this world. It means to be separate—not necessarily physically, but spiritually. We must be careful not to tangle our branches or they will not produce much fruit, and we will not obey the first commandment. The fruit of faith is produced in us as from an active, ongoing relationship with our Vine, Jesus.

Chapter 4
Sin, Disease, and Pruning

Since in the last chapter we examined what faith is, we should examine what its opposite is as well. Paul said in Romans 14:23, "Whatsoever is not of faith is sin," so sin is the opposite of faith. Whenever we fail to trust God, it is sin, and sin is a lack of the fruit of faith. In fact, all sin results from not trusting in God. Remember that "without faith it is impossible to please him"; therefore, only faith pleases God. *The first definition of sin is not trusting God.*

Many might define sin as breaking one of the Ten Commandments from Exodus 20. This is true in part, but breaking any of the commandments is the result of not trusting God. For example, we steal because we do not trust God to provide for us and we murder because we do not trust God to take revenge for us ("For it is written, Vengeance is mine, I will repay, saith the Lord"—Rom. 12:19). In fact, we even covet because we do not trust God to know what is best for us. All actions of disobedience (sin) stem from not trusting or believing God.

Some think of sin as gross aberrations in behavior such as murder, sodomy, and larceny, yet sin is the inward thought even without the outward action. It is an issue of the heart long before the behavior occurs. Jesus said, "Ye have heard that it was said by them of old time, Thou shalt not commit adultery: But I say unto you, That whosoever looketh on a woman to lust after her hath committed adultery with her already in his heart" (Matt. 5:27–28). How can we be guilty of sin without an action? In the kingdom of God, it is our hearts that condemn us, not our actions (1 John 3:20–21). "The LORD searcheth all hearts" (1 Chron. 28:9; see also 1 Sam. 16:7; 1 Kings 8:39; Luke 16:15), and He looks for faith. This is why God was so pleased with King David (Acts 13:22) despite his horrible crimes of adultery and murder (2 Sam. 11).

The simple verse "The just shall live by his faith" (Hab. 2:4) stirred the hearts of Martin Luther and William Tyndale to fuel the Reformation fires of nearly five hundred years ago. Faith is a relationship, which begins and exists in our hearts, not our outward actions. The world can look only at the behavior and therefore has to judge sin as breaking some kind of law like the Ten Commandments. No matter how good our behavior, though, only faith pleases God, and without it all our actions are sin. We must stop comparing our actions to those of other people, including those who claim the name of Christ, and start comparing our hearts to that of the Lord Jesus. Beloved, do not be deceived: "Whatsoever is not of faith is sin."

Rebellion as Sin

In addition, sin is rebellion. This rebellion, which stems from not trusting, begins as all sins do—in the heart—before being manifested in action. A soldier's rebellion toward his commander will begin as a lack of faith or trust in his superior's decisions. The soldier might think *I could do better* for a long time before revealing his rebellious heart to another, and he would probably wait even longer before manifesting the actions necessary to seize command. Yet the rebellion or sin existed in his heart when he stopped trusting his commander. He was deceiving all those around him (like a wolf in sheep's clothing) by his seeming faith, and all his outward obedience to his commander was actually sin because inside he did not trust him.

In the same way, Judas Iscariot did not trust Christ and was in rebellion to Christ long before he betrayed Him. Judas probably followed the Lord outwardly because of Jesus' initial popularity with the people (Matt. 4:24) and because he got to carry the moneybag for the disciples, from which he frequently stole (John 12:6). In fact, Judas's behavior totally deceived the other disciples until the betrayal (John 13:29), but it did not fool Jesus.

The Lord is never fooled by one's behavior, for He looks at the heart. Judas's heart did not have faith in Christ and was therefore full of sin. When the time for His betrayal came, "Said Jesus unto him, That thou doest, do quickly" (John 13:27). Whether it is children not trusting their parents, a soldier not trusting his superior, Judas not trusting Jesus, or us not trusting Christ, God describes this inward lack of faith as rebellion or sin: "Take heed, brethren, lest there be in any of you an evil heart of unbelief" (Heb. 3:12).

Fruitlessness As Sin

Paul gave another definition of sin in his letter to the Romans: "For all have sinned, and come short of the glory of God" (Rom. 3:23). In this verse, Paul was implying that sin is anything that falls short of God's glory. The Greek word from which sin is derived, *hamartia*, is an archery term that literally means "to miss the mark." Just like the archer who makes a tremendous effort yet misses the bulls-eye, when we come short of His glory, it is sin. And what is God's glory or the mark we must hit with the arrow? It is fruitfulness. Remember Jesus said that the Father is glorified when we bear fruit (John 15:8). Being fruitful and multiplying, fulfilling the first commandment, achieves the glory of God, and if sin is coming short of His glory, then sin can again be defined as not bearing fruit.

Yielding the fruit of the Spirit glorifies God, and "against such there is no law" (Gal. 5:23). Man's laws or standards cannot judge the fruit of the Spirit; only God's Spirit can judge them: "But if ye be led of the Spirit, ye are not under the law" (Gal. 5:18). These fruits reveal the true heart and the presence of God's Spirit (Matt. 7:20), and it is these fruits that please God; all else is sin. In fact, sin is not only the opposite of faith, but also the opposite of all the fruits. In speaking His first words to us, "Be fruitful, and multiply," God was telling us not to sin.

Obviously, bearing poison fruit is sin as well. Many believe that sin is to "fulfil the lust of the flesh" (Gal. 5:16), and that the list of "the works of the flesh" from Galatians 5:19–21 translates into a litany of sin. This is true. These fleshly works, which we earlier referred to as "poison" or evil fruits, are the opposite of the fruit of the Spirit. All sin comes from not yielding good fruit. Living in sin is actually living with poison fruit and not exhibiting the fruit of the Spirit.

The Judgment of Sin

Since sin is not yielding the fruit of the Spirit, then to be consistent, the judgment of sin must be the same as the judgment of the branch that does not bear fruit. Paul wrote, "The wages of sin is death" (Rom. 6:23). Furthermore, James 1:15 says, "When lust hast conceived, it bringeth forth sin: and sin, when it is finished, bringeth forth death."

While the judgment of sin is clearly death, the judgment of not bearing fruit is much the same. As we've noted in pre-

vious chapters, Jesus said that every tree refusing to bear good
fruit will be cut down and burned (Matt. 7:19). In John
15:2, He put it this way: "Every branch in me that beareth
not fruit he taketh away." Where does He "taketh away" the
branch? Jesus continued, "If a man abide not in me, he is cast
forth as a branch, and is withered; and men gather them, and
cast them into the fire, and they are burned" (v. 6). Fruitless
branches face the fires of destruction (Rev. 20:15). *Sin is not
bearing fruit.*

Disease and Pruning

One reason that farmers cut off branches from fruitless trees
is that they often are diseased. Fruit-bearing vines have fragile
members, and there are a myriad of diseases, called blights,
that can affect them. Once disease enters a branch, if left
untreated, it will spread throughout the branch and kill it; it
may spread to other branches as well. The effects can be devastating and often require drastic measures.

The spiritual picture these blights represent is sin. As disease
destroys us physically, a little at a time, so sin devastates us spiritually. The disease of sin, though it may start small, can spread
and affect other areas of our lives as well until death occurs.
Actually, sin may result in physical illness. Paul wrote, "For this
cause many are weak and sickly among you" (1 Cor. 11:30).

The treatment for a diseased branch or sinful believer is
purging. Jesus said, "Every branch that beareth fruit, He pur-

geth it, that it may bring forth more fruit" (John 15:2). The Greek word translated "purgeth" in this verse is *kathairo* and literally means "to take down" or "to cleanse." Many modern translations actually use "prune" instead of "purgeth." Pruning removes the diseased part of a branch and prevents the blight from spreading, thus cleansing and saving the branch, and preparing it to bear fruit.

Just like a branch, we must allow God to prune the parts of our lives that cause us to sin or not produce fruit. Jesus said:

> If thy hand offend thee, cut it off: it is better for thee to enter into life maimed, than having two hands to go into hell, into the fire that never shall be quenched . . . And if thy foot offend thee, cut it off: it is better for thee to enter halt into life, than having two feet to be cast into hell, into the fire that never shall be quenched . . . And if thine eye offend thee, pluck it out: it is better for thee to enter into the kingdom of God with one eye, than having two eyes to be cast into hell fire: Where their worm dieth not, and the fire is not quenched. (Mark 9:43,45,47– 48)

We should not literally remove our hand or foot or eye, but we should take serious action against the areas of our life that do not produce fruit. This is pruning.

The passage I've just quoted pictures the destruction of the flesh. Both fire and worms destroy the flesh, but in this passage Jesus spoke of a perpetual (everlasting) destruction or torment. He was actually referring to the last verse in Isaiah; "And they shall go forth, and look upon the carcasses of the men that have transgressed against me: for their worm shall not die, neither shall their fire be quenched; and they shall be an abhorring unto all flesh" (66:24). This is an eternal consumption of the flesh; thus, we must allow God to prune the problem areas out of our lives before we face the grave with the fire and the worms (judgment). As we can see, Jesus spoke strongly against sin and fruitlessness.

The Eternal Benefits of Pruning

A while back, our county extension agent came out and taught me how to trim the various fruit trees on my farm. He explained that pruning would allow more sunlight to reach the middle of the plant so the maximum number of leaves could collect light. (In Scripture, the sun represents the Lord Jesus—Ps. 19:5–6; Rev. 1:16). The extension agent said that I should not allow any areas of the branch to be shaded by other parts, for the areas of the branch that do not get enough light are very prone to blight. By pruning the parts of the branch that block light from other parts, I actually help the whole tree resist disease.

It is the same in the life of the Christian. Sin tends to enter our lives through areas that are not in God's light.

These are the areas of our lives that may not appear diseased yet are in rebellion to the Lord Jesus, and these areas do not produce fruit. These are activities and behaviors that we rationalize and justify as "good" based on worldly wisdom.

In fact, many Christians need to prune what others would consider wholesome activities because they are too busy to spend time with God. Relationships take time, and some even need to prune church activities or ministry work because they are too occupied with them, and they are not bearing fruit. The "fruit of the womb" (children) does not usually come from the wife spending time with her brothers and sisters; a child comes from the wife spending time alone with her husband. And so it is with our Husband, the Lord Jesus.

Remember, these activities are not necessarily embarrassing and often appear pious, yet they are sin and prevent us from "having a good conscience" (1 Pet. 3:15–16) before God. As we prune these things out of our lives (those "shady" or shade-causing parts of the branch) then we remove potential disease (sin).

Another reason for pruning is so that the nutrients and the resources of the vine are not wasted on fruitless parts of the branch. Similarly, we must be careful not to waste our resources, such as time and finances, on activities, organizations, and relationships that do not bear fruit. We must redeem the time (Eph. 5:16) and be good stewards of what God has provided for us. By pruning these unnecessary activities and behaviors out of our lives, we allow our "branch" to bear the maximum amount of love, joy, peace, and other fruits of the Spirit. In time, sin, rebellion, or unfaithfulness (disease) will creep back into our hearts, but as God's light shines on our branch, His Spirit will reveal what we need to prune.

Pruning begins with confession: "If we confess our sins, he is faithful and just to forgive us our sins, and to cleanse us from all unrighteousness" (1 John 1:9). The word "cleanse" in this verse is *katharizo* and is obviously related to *kathairo*. Thus, it is by confession that God "purgeth it, that it may bring forth more fruit" (John 15:2).

Faith's opposite is sin; when we express our trust (faith) in God, we are bearing fruit. Those branches with poison fruit (sin) need trimming so they may eventually bear good fruit. This allows us to fulfill the first commandment. When the harvest comes, will we have any fruit? Only skillful pruning will tell.

Chapter 5
Men As Trees

We have seen how the Bible pictures children of God abiding in the true Vine, Jesus. In addition, we have read that the children of God represent grain-producing plants such as wheat in the parable of the sower. The branches of the vine and the wheat plants are to fulfill the first commandment by producing fruit or grain. In the case of the vine, the seed is in the fruit, and in the example of wheat, the seed is the fruit, and as the seed or grain is scattered, multiplying occurs. The Seed is Jesus, and only the "good ground," representing a good heart, fulfilled the first commandment "and did yield fruit that sprang up and increased" (Mark 4:8).

As we proceed, we need to examine more closely the depiction from Scripture in which men are represented as fruit-bearing trees. We glanced at this truth in the last chapter, but I'd like to study it more intensely here.

King David had a revelation of men being trees when he began the book of Psalms.

> Blessed is the man that walketh not in the counsel
> of the ungodly, nor standeth in the way of sin-
> ners, nor sitteth in the seat of the scornful. But
> his delight is in the law of the LORD; and in his
> law doth he meditate day and night. And he shall
> be like a tree planted by the rivers of water, that
> bringeth forth his fruit in his season; his leaf also
> shall not wither; and whatsoever he doeth shall
> prosper. (Psalm 1:1–3)

If a man delights himself in the law of God, which he demonstrates by meditating on God's Word day and night, he will not only be a tree, but a tree planted by rivers of water. God desires His "trees," His children, to bear His fruit. As we consider and think about God's Word, our tree will receive ample water, which produces a greater yield of fruit.

This passage identifies three types of individuals who do not bear fruit. The first is a man who lives "in the counsel of the ungodly." He represents those who believe and make decisions based on the lies of this world. These "trees" will not bear the fruit of God's Spirit, for they do not abide in God. The second group includes those who stand in the path or "way of sinners." These will not bear fruit either, for they trust in the "way" of the world, not the Lord. The third group comprises men who sit in the "seat of the scornful"; their "trees" will produce only poison fruits that result in scorn (mocking with contempt).

Avoid the Seat of Scorn

This last is particularly dangerous. God desires our "tree" to bear His fruit of meekness, not the poison of arrogance, and He will exalt us in His time. "Humble [become meek] yourselves in the sight of the Lord, and he shall lift you up" (James 4:10). We should not sit in this seat of judging others.

It is interesting that the Hebrew word translated "scornful" is *loots*, which is also translated as "interpreters," "teachers," and even "ambassadors" in other Old Testament verses. Could this "seat of the scornful" be "Moses' seat" and the "chief seats in the synagogues" that Jesus accused the ambitious Pharisees of desiring (Matt. 23:1–9)? These Pharisees loved to sit in front of the congregation of Israel and act as "interpreters" (*loots*) of the Scripture and "teach" (*loots*) "for doctrines the commandments of men" (Matt. 15:9). From this seat, these Pharisees poured out their "scorn" (*loots*) and derided (mocked or judged) those who did not agree and follow. These leaders convinced the congregations over time that Scripture gave them authority over the assembly and that their sect possessed the "true" doctrines and traditions (as opposed to those of the Sadducees and others).

Sometimes the Bible uses "interpreter" (*loots*) to describe more of an intermediary or mediator. The Pharisees of Jesus' day, as many such men through history, sought the seat of interpreter and teacher to gain the powerful position of mediator over the people, and it is from this position that they even planned to kill Jesus (Matt. 26:3–4), the true Mediator between God and men. Of course, they killed Jesus in the name of God, and present-day "Pharisees" will do the same to us today in the name of Jesus if we threaten their position. We must remain meek and avoid the "seat of the scornful" as well as those who sit in it today.

Be Ye Meek

Another example of Scripture representing men as trees occurred when God spoke to Israel through Jotham in Judges 9.

> The trees went forth on a time to anoint a king
> over them; and they said unto the olive tree,
> Reign thou over us. But the olive tree said unto
> them, Should I leave my fatness, wherewith by
> me they honour God and man, and go to be pro-
> moted over the trees? And the trees said to the fig
> tree, Come thou, and reign over us. But the fig
> tree said unto them, Should I forsake my sweet-
> ness, and my good fruit, and go to be promoted
> over the trees? Then said the trees unto the vine,
> Come thou, and reign over us. And the vine said
> unto them, Should I leave my wine, which

cheereth God and man, and go to be promoted
over the trees? Then said all the trees unto the
bramble, Come thou, and reign over us. And the
bramble said unto the trees, If in truth ye anoint
me king over you, then come and put your trust
in my shadow: and if not, let fire come out of the
bramble, and devour the cedars of Lebanon.
(Judges 9:8–15)

In this passage, the fruit-bearing plants (olive tree, fig tree,
and grapevine) refused to give up their primary directive of
being fruitful to become king. For example, the vine would not
leave producing wine. "Wine maketh merry" (Eccl. 10:19) the
hearts of men, and also "cheereth God" (Judg. 9:13). Wine
comes from fruit. God desires "wine," and the world will know
us by our fruit.

*We must realize that the true trees of God are not interested in
a promotion by man.* As His trees, we should desire only the
fruit of meekness (humility) and be cautious of ambition. We
should know that God will exalt us through fruit and not seek
elevation by men or organizations.

Now the bramble (thorns) could not produce fruit, yet it
was willing to lead, under one condition: "And the bramble said
unto the trees, If in truth ye anoint me king over you, then come
and put your trust in my shadow" (v. 15). The bramble wanted
the other trees to follow and trust in him and not God.
Ambitious people who seek to lead men and build bigger organi-

zations may not be trusting God, and we can tell because as the bramble they do not produce fruit. Even if they come in the name of Jesus, they must produce spiritual fruit to be of God.

Just like the bramble or thornbush, men who desire to lead you spiritually can be treacherous. If they want you to "put your trust in [their] shadow[s]," beware. So many through history have led others to commit unspeakable atrocities in the name of Jesus. We must have our own relationships with the Vine and not abide in other "branches." We must beware the subtle deception that we need some person (in addition to Christ) to be our mediator with God.

Remember, God chooses His leaders from the humble. He selected Moses to lead Israel because he was meekest (Num. 12:3), and Isaiah said that in the kingdom of God "a little child shall lead them" (Isa. 11:6). Daniel 4:17 says that God uses the "basest of men" (the meekest) to lead in the kingdom of God.

Isaiah and Mark's Take on Trees

Isaiah also experienced revelations of men appearing as trees. One of these says that men "might be called trees of righteousness, the planting of the LORD, that he might be glorified" (Isa. 61:3). The Lord plants Jesus the Seed in us, and He yields in us the tree of life. As we produce the fruit of the Spirit, we are "called trees of righteousness," and again in this is our Father glorified.

A New Testament writer, Mark, included a reference to men as trees.

> And [Jesus] cometh to Bethsaida: and they bring
> a blind man unto him, and besought him to
> touch him. And he took the blind man by the
> hand, and led him out of the town; and when he
> had spit on his eyes, and put his hands upon him,
> he asked him if he saw ought. And he looked up,
> and said, I see men as trees, walking. After that he
> put his hands again upon his eyes, and made him
> look up: and he was restored, and saw every man
> clearly. (Mark 8:22–25)

I found it so interesting that in the transition of the man receiving his sight, he saw something others could not see. Was this vision of men being trees a revelation from God just like those of Jotham, David, and Isaiah? Some interpret this passage as saying that the man's sight was just initially blurry—in his not-yet-fully-restored vision, men looked like trees. If this is the case, why did Mark record this detail? Why did Jesus ask the man what he saw? And note that the man described trees, not fuzzy shapes. It is possible the man had been blind from birth; if so, how could he have known what trees looked like? The man clearly saw men represented as trees, and Jesus made sure this statement appeared in Mark's gospel.

Jesus said, "I am come into this world, that they which see not might see; and that they which see might be made blind" (John 9:39). I pray that power, pride, and traditions do not blind us.

Two Trees in the Field

We have roughly seen that there are two types of trees: those that abide by the water and produce fruit, or "good trees," and those that produce poison fruit, or corrupt trees. In nature God created two types of trees as well.

Genesis 2:9 says, "And out of the ground made the LORD God to grow every tree that is pleasant to the sight, and good for food." In a general sense, there are trees that are "good for food" and produce fruit, and there are trees that are "pleasant to the sight" and are useful for other purposes.

Fruit-producing trees are generally unattractive, especially after years of pruning. In fact, nothing would draw you to these trees except their fruit. They are often short and ineffective as shade cover, and their wood is not good for lumber. Actually, without proper pruning they are not much use at all.

In addition, fruit-producing trees have soft, flexible boughs that bend and move with the wind. Jesus said, "The wind bloweth where it listeth [desires], and thou hearest the sound thereof, but canst not tell whence it cometh, and whither it goeth: so is every one that is born of the Spirit" (John 3:8). *Just as the fruit trees have branches that bend as the wind blows them, we, too, are to be pliable when the Spirit moves us.* Remember, the Greek word *pneuma* is translated both "wind" and "spirit." We are to be pliant in yielding to the Spirit of God just as the fruit tree gives way to the wind.

Unlike fruit trees, the trees that are "pleasant to the sight" are tall, strong, and appear in Scripture as cedars, oaks, and even the cypress. Bible authors compared these hardy trees to worldly kings and kingdoms of the Old Testament such as Assyria (Ezek. 31) and Nebuchadnezzar (Dan. 4), as well as rebellious Judah (Ezek. 17).

These powerful, towering trees grow straight and provide shade for the birds of the air, which nest in their branches, and shelter in which the beast of the field can find rest (Dan. 14). These trees provide lumber for the projects that men conceive, and it is from them that men have built their palaces and fortresses. These trees are beautiful and often require no pruning. In contrast to the easily bent fruit trees, the cedar and oak stand firm against the wind. In fact, they are rigid, and if you push them too hard, they will just break.

This picture in nature is quite striking: the oaks and cedars are tall (proud) and stiff (resistant to change), whereas the fruit-producing trees are small (humble) and flexible, allowing themselves to be moved by the wind (Spirit).

Strength and Beauty Aren't Everything

While the fruit-producing trees—or children of the kingdom—are generally unattractive, they do fulfill the first commandment, and this was true of the Lord Jesus. Isaiah 53:2 says, "He hath no form nor comeliness [beauty or splendor]; and when we shall see him, there is no beauty that we should desire him." Jesus was like the humble fruit tree in that there was nothing in His appearance to attract people to Him. He was totally flexible in the "wind" (Spirit) in that He did only the will of His Father. Many today fuss over their looks or behavior in order attract or impress others (as the Pharisees did), but let me say it again: "By their fruits ye shall know them" (Matt. 7:20).

Ezekiel 31 compares the Assyrian kingdom to a cedar in Lebanon, a majestic, elegant tree whose height,

> "was exalted above all the trees of the field,
> and his boughs were multiplied, and his branches
> became long . . . All the fowls of heaven made
> their nests in his boughs, and under his branches
> did all the beasts of the field bring forth their
> young, and under shadow dwelt all great nations.
> Thus was he fair in his greatness (vv. 5–7)

The Lord saw the arrogance of this "tree" and responded:

> "Because thou hast lifted up thyself in height,
> and he hath shot up his top among the thick
> boughs, and his heart is lifted up in his height;
> I have therefore delivered him into the hand of

the mighty one of the heathen [Satan]; he shall
surely deal with him: I have driven him out for
his wickedness (vv. 10–11).

The cedar grew taller than even the trees in the garden of
God because of His blessing. But the tree exalted itself with
pride, and God destroyed it. Even though this tree had glory
like the trees of Eden, the Lord brought it down "unto the
nether parts of the earth [hell]" (v. 18).

Just as the seed from the fruit trees brings forth only trees
"after [their] kind" (Gen. 1:11), the seeds of oaks and cedars
bring forth only trees "after their kind": rigid, proud trees that
stand tall and call attention to themselves. The cedar and oak
may appear early on as fruit trees, but they produce poison
fruits. They may appear as children of God, but the difference, as always, is in the fruit.

In addition, fruit-bearing trees are more fragile than
cedars or oaks and so more easily become diseased. Oaks and
cedars are very resistant to blights. It is the same in the kingdom of God, and the diagnosis is sin. Children of God are
much more susceptible to the disease of sin than the children
of the world, who are often ignorant of their sin and thus
less affected.

Instead of examining themselves in God's light, these
Christians compare themselves to the world. These people
long to be pleasant to the eye, and they may stand strong and
rigid (like cedars and oaks) as they reach toward heaven to

show off their good works. But we know what the result will be: "Every tree that bringeth not forth good fruit is hewn down, and cast into the fire" (Matt. 7:19). Yes, the children of this world may not be affected as much by sin in this physical life, but their end is doom, "the pit" (Ezek. 31:16).

Humility is a fruit, and if we are to be trees, then we should be like the fruit-bearing trees planted next to living water—like flexible trees that move at the Spirit's command. We should not have our own ambition but in meekness seek only the Father's will, to fulfill the first commandment: "*Parah rabah.*"

Chapter 6
Two Trees in Eden: Life and Death

We have dwelled longer on the trees than on any other topic, and this is because they have so much more to teach us. And Jesus taught using the tree metaphor again and again, because it was something with which His audience was familiar. So as you read, picture yourself living in a culture that existed long before ours in the twenty-first century; discover the importance of the distinctions between tree types and how they can help you better understand yourself and your weaknesses.

While God likens men to trees in the Scripture and created generally two types of trees in nature, it is no accident that there were also two trees in the midst of the Garden of Eden: "And the LORD God planted a garden eastward in Eden; and . . . out of the ground made the LORD God to grow every tree that is pleasant to the sight, and good for food; the tree of life also in the midst of the garden, and the tree of knowledge of good and evil" (Gen. 2:8–9). These two trees can give us much understanding of the disobedience and foolishness of men and God's provision in Jesus Christ.

Adam and Eve lived in this perfect garden that God had planted just for them. They dwelt with "the tree of life, which is in the midst of the paradise of God" (Rev. 2:7), and they had no guilt or shame. Their Father had created them physically as well as spiritually: "And the LORD God formed man of the dust of the ground [physical existence], and breathed into his nostrils the breath of life [spiritual existence]; and man became a living soul" (Gen. 2:7).

In Hebrew, the word for "breath" in this verse can also mean "spirit" (similar to the Greek word *pneuma*), and this suggests that God breathed into Adam the spirit of life. No matter what theological term one wants to use, this spirit or breath of life is probably what distinguishes us from the animals in creation.

Now, Adam and Eve were able to eat from any tree of the garden they desired except for the tree of the knowledge of good and evil: "For in the day that thou eatest thereof thou shalt surely die," their Creator told them (Gen. 2:17). If eating from this tree caused one to die, then this was the tree of death. Therefore, in the middle of the Garden of Eden were the tree of life and the tree of death.

Death—but Not Physical

In Genesis 3, Eve, being deceived by the serpent, ate of the tree of the knowledge of good and evil (tree of death), as did her husband. The result was that they then had shame and guilt. In addition, they, as well as their future descendants, were cursed (Gen. 3:14–19), but they did not die physically. In fact, Eve later had children, and Adam lived for a total of 930 years. Yet God had clearly said, "For in the day that thou eatest thereof thou shalt surely die." What happened?

Adam and Eve did not die physically that day; they died spiritually. And when Adam died spiritually, all of us who were his future descendants—all humanity to come—did so that day as well. If physical death separates us from the kingdoms of this world, then spiritual death separates us from the kingdom of God. When Adam and Eve ate from the tree of death, they left the kingdom of God and started the kingdoms of this world.

Not only is death the removal of life, but eating from the tree of death also caused removal from the tree of life. As a consequence of Adam's disobedience, God banished him from the paradise of Eden to ensure that he and his descendants would not eat from the tree of life (Gen. 3:24) while he was under this curse, in his current state of "death." *In heaven, however, we will get to eat again from the tree of life* (Rev. 2:7). Although Adam is removed from the tree of life at the beginning of the Bible, we are again living with the tree of life in the end of the book. Therefore, something must happen in the interim. Somehow we are to come alive spiritually and enter again into the kingdom of God.

Jesus described this coming alive spiritually: "Verily, verily, I say unto thee, except a man be born again, he cannot see the kingdom of God" (John 3:3). This second birth is a spiritual birth of God's Spirit in us, while the first birth is only the physical birth of our flesh. Jesus continued, "That which is born of the flesh is flesh; and that which is born of the Spirit is spirit. Marvel not that I said unto thee, ye must be born again" (vv. 6–7).

Paul explained, "For since by man [Adam] came death, by man [Jesus] came also the resurrection of the dead. For as in Adam all die, even so in Christ shall all be made alive" (1 Cor. 15:21–22). Just as we all died spiritually in the Garden of Eden with Adam because of his disobedience, we can be born again spiritually (resurrected) with Christ because of His obedience.

When Adam ate the fruit from the tree of the knowledge of good and evil (tree of death), he received the seed from that tree and passed this seed on to all his future generations. Just as the good fruits on the tree of life have the incorruptible Seed who is Jesus, the poison fruits on the corrupt tree of the knowledge of good and evil have the corruptible seed that came from Adam. This corruptible seed passes from the father (not the mother) to the children in the form of a curse. As we receive this seed or curse from our fathers, the tree of death begins to grow in us, and we yield the poison fruit of the flesh on a daily basis.

Adam came under the curse because of rebellion (sin), and he could produce only children under the curse "after his own kind." As descendants of Adam, we all have this curse of sin in us, and we all now have this evil, corrupt tree growing in our hearts.

There were two trees in the garden of God: the tree of life that represented Christ, and the tree of the knowledge of good and evil that represented Adam and his seed. The tree of life has good fruit with incorruptible seed, while the tree of death has poison fruit with corruptible seed.

Two Trees: Curse and Cure

In the Garden of Eden, the tree of death brought devastating consequences to Adam and his descendants. Eating the poison fruit produced death and the curse, and therefore the tree of the knowledge of good and evil is also the tree of the curse. Since the only cure for death is life, then the tree of life is also the tree of the cure. John the apostle said, referring to the tree of life, "The leaves of the tree were for the healing [curing] of the nations. And there shall be no more curse" (Rev. 22:2–3).

Adam's cursed state, after he ate the poison fruit (called the fall of man), had several consequences for mankind. First, Adam and his descendants would then think first of themselves or be self-centered. All men are predetermined to be concerned about themselves (or their close relations) over others. We cannot help it; it is in our seed. It is the curse of the tree of death.

In contrast, the tree of life allows us to "Love [our] neighbour as [ourselves]" (Matt. 19:19). Sure, we often go to great lengths to appear concerned about others, but inside we are often like the Pharisees who desired the approval of man. In fact, because of rationalization, we often deceive ourselves and believe we are pleasing to God. This is why Jesus said we must perform our benevolent acts and say our prayers in private or secret (Matt. 6:1–6), because this is the only way to know we do not desire men's approval.

Second, the curse placed all mankind in the bondage of the fear of death. Before Adam's disobedience or sin, he had no concept of a physical end to his life. But God said, "Dust thou art, and unto dust shalt thou return" (Gen. 3:19), and consequently we are all dying of an incurable disease called physical existence. The fear of death often controls us. Since Satan holds the "power of [physical] death," we are "them that through fear of death were all their lifetime subject to bondage" (Heb. 2:14–15).

Revelation refers to "Satan, which deceiveth the whole world" (Rev. 12:9), for you see, if we viewed ourselves (by faith) as eternal beings, we would not fear death, and we could focus on others. If we truly understood that our few years in this life are immeasurable next to eternity, we would spend this time serving those who do not understand, instead of serving ourselves. And we would be free of the fear of death (Ps. 68:20; Isa. 25:8; 1 Cor. 15:54–57).

As a third result of the curse, Adam no longer walked with God and trusted Him from an intimate relationship (covenant), but he became as God, judging good and evil for himself (Gen. 3:22). Adam could not help but act this way because this was part of the curse from the eating of that tree. As Adam's descendants, we are now bound until our physical deaths to trust in ourselves and not in God.

If we are bound not to trust God, and not trusting is sin, then we are bound to sin. This is what Paul meant when he said, "O wretched man that I am! Who shall deliver me from the body of this death?" (Rom. 7:24) Paul realized that he was under the curse of Adam and that he had no power to release himself. He was destined to follow his own understanding of good and evil until he returned to the dust of the ground.

A common, modern-day lie is that man is born good and his environment makes him evil. This is not true. Man is born evil under the curse from the seed of the corrupt tree, and training is required to make him do good. For those of you who have children, do they ever deceive, mislead, or disobey in any way? If the answer is yes, then who taught them to do evil? Did you teach them to lie or disobey? Of course not. They behave this way because of the curse or seed within them. They may not even realize they lie; they may just instinctively do so to get their way and escape consequences.

Do your children naturally want to serve others, or would they rather be served? Like most adults, they probably prefer the latter. Yet again through discipline, we can train children to serve others. (Unfortunately, even if you train your children to do good, tell the truth, and serve others, through no fault of your own, your children's children will demonstrate the evil behavior anew in the next generation. It is in their seed.)

Actually, training alone is hopeless. Even if you train your children to choose good over evil, this will not make them spiritual and will not give them eternal life. If out of their own understanding they choose good, they will still be trusting in their own understanding and not God. Sure, choosing good is much more acceptable and beneficial to society than choosing evil, but if we are trusting in our understanding of good and evil and not God's, then we are still eating from the tree of curse or death, not the tree of cure or life. Our children must receive the Seed (Jesus) of the tree of life to be cured of the curse and enter the kingdom of God. They must be born a second time.

Two Trees: Flesh and Spirit

This second birth, as we've said, is a spiritual birth. When we were born physically, we received the cursed seed from Adam and produced the poison fruits (or works) of the flesh listed in Galatians 5:19–21. Thus, the tree of the curse or death is also the tree of the flesh. We are born of the flesh, or rather the tree of the flesh, in our physical birth.

But when we are born again, we are born of the Spirit by receiving the Seed from the tree of life. Therefore, this tree of life is also the tree of the Spirit. As the tree of flesh yields the fruit of the flesh, the tree of the Spirit produces the fruit of the Spirit, and yields spiritual seed for multiplying.

As we walk with this tree of the Spirit, we are walking with God. "This I say then, Walk in the Spirit, and ye shall not fulfil the lust [works or poison fruits] of the flesh" (Gal. 5:16).

Two Trees: Law and Faith

In the middle of the Garden of Eden were two trees: the trees of death and life, the trees of curse and cure, and the trees of flesh and Spirit. These two trees were also the trees of law and faith. Paul said, "The letter [of the law] killeth, but the spirit giveth life" (2 Cor. 3:6). If the law brings death, then the law is from the tree of death and thus is the tree of law. This verse implies that law is the opposite of Spirit, but law is also the opposite of faith: "No man is justified by the law in the sight of God, it is evident: for, The just shall live by faith. And the law is not of faith: but, The man that doeth them shall live in them" (Gal. 3:11–12). If we are to live by faith, then faith gives life, thus the tree of life is the tree of faith. Just as faith is the opposite of sin, faith is the opposite of law. In fact, living solely under the law is living in sin. It is missing the mark, and it brings death.

How can this be? How can living by and keeping God's law bring death? Did not David write, "The law of the Lord is perfect, converting the soul" (Ps. 19:7)? How can this "perfect" law that converts the soul bring death? *God's law in itself is not the result of a curse, nor does it bring death, but it is man's trusting in his own understanding of God's law and judging others by this that brings death.* God's law converts our souls and gives life, but because of the curse, we tend to trust in our version of God's law—as the Pharisees did—and we use our interpretation to critique and judge others.

It is so important that we understand that, again, God's law does not bring death or bondage by itself. It *is* perfect, bringing freedom and life. The law brings death only when man walks in his own understanding of God's law and uses it to abuse others rather than judge himself (1 Cor. 11:31–32), which brings life.

Free from the Tree

What will set us free from the bondage of this tree of death? Galatians 3:13 says, "Christ hath redeemed us from the curse of the law, being made a curse for us: for it is written, Cursed is every one that hangeth on a tree." The glorious cross on which our Lord Jesus died was the tree of the knowledge of good and evil, the tree of death, the tree of the curse, the tree of the flesh, and the tree of law. Jesus was bound (nailed) to the tree of the curse (cross) for Adam's (and our) disobedience to free us from the tree of the knowledge of good and evil. Only through the cross of Christ can man find freedom from bondage to his own desire to be God and make decisions for himself: "If the Son therefore shall make you free, ye shall be free indeed" (John 8:36).

Furthermore, in our freedom we again have the right to eat from the tree of life in the garden of God so that we may manifest those twelve fruits of the Spirit that the tree of life produces.

> There is therefore now no condemnation to them which are in Christ Jesus, who walk not after the flesh [their own desires], but after the Spirit. For the [new] law of the Spirit of [tree of] life in Christ Jesus hath made me free from the law [tree] of sin and death, (Romans 8:1–2)

The Good Side of a Bad Tree

Once Christ has set us free from the tree of the knowledge of good and evil and we are able to eat from the tree of life, an interesting thing happens. When we came to Christ, we were in bondage to Satan, and we were eating from the evil side of the tree. The law of God convicted us of our evil deeds, and we repented. Now as we begin to grow, Satan begins to show us the "good" side of the tree of death instead of the evil side in an effort to keep us eating from it. Instead of our continuing in evil deeds, he suggests that we now replace them with good deeds. These good deeds, however, arise still from our own understanding, not God's, of what good is. These works disguise our guilt and cause us to forget our conviction as we begin to exalt ourselves because of our "worthy" actions. But these deeds are still dead and do not give life.

There are many today who have the power to be free from the curse but remain at the wrong tree. Paul said, "Are ye so foolish? Having begun in the Spirit, are ye now made perfect by the flesh?" (Gal. 3:3) We now cling to "good" behavior and morals, and we even train our children to do the same. Yet we remain self-centered, self-absorbed, trying to perfect our outward actions before men while our inward man remains in bondage to the flesh, the fear of death, the wrong tree, and of course, Satan.

Many say we should pray for revival, but if we develop a closer and more trusting relationship with our Father, then revival will come. In the model prayer of Jesus, referred to as the Lord's Prayer, He did not pray for revival. He prayed for the will of God to be done on earth, and His will is that we believe (trust) in the one He sent, Jesus (John 6:29).

"The just shall live by faith," and faith is one of the fruits on the tree of life. This tree is also called the tree of cure, the tree of the Spirit, the tree of faith, and it is represented in nature as fruit-bearing trees. The other tree is the tree of man's judgment (good and evil), also called the tree of death, the tree of curse, the tree of the flesh, the tree of law, the tree of sin, and it is represented in nature by the stately cedars and oaks. Most important, this evil tree was the cross of Christ through which He conquered the curse, the flesh, sin, and even death.

Two trees in God's garden; two trees in earth's fields today. When the Farmer checks His harvest, will He find homely but highly fruitful trees that give Him pleasure—or beautiful and brash trees that bring Him pain? Will we seek to be intimate with God and fulfill the first commandment? The choice is, as always, ours.

Chapter 7
Two Covenants

Just as the two trees in the Garden of Eden symbolize life and death, Spirit and flesh, cure and curse, law and faith, and the trees of the field, they also represent two covenants. The tree of the knowledge of good and evil represents the old covenant that God gave through Moses at Mount Sinai. The tree of life is a relationship with Jesus Christ through the new covenant. We proclaim this new covenant or testament as we partake of the Lord's Supper: the bread (crushed fruit of the grain) symbolizes His flesh, and wine (crushed fruit of the vine) represents His blood.

This old covenant of law is for those who do not want a relationship with God, but like the Pharisees, just desire proper outward behavior. This is analogous to the Israelites at Mount Sinai. In Exodus 20, we have the Ten Commandments (vv. 3–17), but the most interesting part of the chapter is in verses 18–21:

> And all the people saw the thunderings, and the
> lightnings, and the noise of the trumpet, and the
> mountain smoking: and when the people saw it,
> they removed, and stood afar off. And they said
> unto Moses, Speak thou with us, and we will
> hear: but let not God speak with us, lest we die.
> And Moses said unto the people, Fear not: for
> God has come to prove you, and that his fear
> may be before your faces, that ye sin not. And
> the people stood afar off, and Moses drew near
> unto the thick darkness where God was.

God wanted an intimate relationship with every one of those Israelites. He wanted every one of them to continue to hear His voice. Consider the Scriptures in which He described Himself as Israel's "husband" (Isa. 54:5; Jer. 31:32)—clearly He desired a personal relationship with them. They just wanted the law. They wanted Moses to teach them as an intermediary, and they did not want God to speak to them directly through a relationship. The Israelites at Mount Sinai were content to come to the assemblies and attempt to keep the rules. The result of their rejection of fellowship with God was the bondage of the law of Moses (Gal. 4:24).

Just like the Israelites at Mount Sinai, we find our relationship with God begins with fear, but we base the continuing connection on hearing His voice. Because of fear, they desired to interact with man (Moses) instead of God. Are we willing to seek Him directly to hear His voice? Or would we rather have a mediator other than Jesus? Hearing His voice may cost everything, even our lives. It may cause us to "fear and quake" as Moses did (Heb. 12:21). God's voice shakes all created things (on earth and in heaven), but the words He speaks cannot be shaken.

The whole purpose of the new covenant is that we no longer require any man to teach us as Moses taught the Israelites. "I will put my law in their inward parts, and write it in their hearts; and will be their God, and they shall be my people" (Jer. 31:33). Jesus is the Mediator of a new covenant in which the Holy Spirit teaches us directly: "The anointing which ye have received of him abideth in you, and ye need not that any man teach you: but the same anointing teacheth you of all things, and is truth, and is no lie, and even as it hath taught you, ye shall abide in him" (1 John 2:27).

We must hear the Master's voice ourselves and respond. "To day if ye will hear his voice, harden not your heart . . . as in the day of temptation in the wilderness" (Ps. 95:7–8). This verse is so important that the writer of Hebrews quoted it three times (3:7–8, 3:15, 4:7). We must not harden our hearts, but search and listen.

Close and Direct

Unfortunately, many today behave as the Israelites did at Mount Sinai. Even though they live in the New Testament era, they still operate under the old covenant and seek a mediator other than Christ. These modern-day Israelites just want to follow the expectations of their churches and their relationships with Christ are very shallow. They seem to say, "Pastor, Bishop, Elder, or Sunday school Teacher, you go spend all week with God, and then you come tell us Sunday morning what He had to say. Yes, we will be there Sunday morning, Sunday night, and Wednesday night, but we do not need a closer relationship. We just want the message. Just let us know what we are supposed to do, but do not change our lives or make us spend time with God. We are too busy; you be our mediator, and you give us His message."

This does not mean we cannot learn from others, for in fact we sometimes hear God through fellow believers. *But we must mainly hear God directly.* I may sometimes send a message to my wife through one of my daughters, but we would have a very superficial relationship if that were how we primarily communicated. Close and deep relationships come from direct communication.

To further illustrate this point, suppose the president invited you to be his friend and travel with him wherever he went. Just think, you would fly around on *Air Force One* and meet different heads of state. You would tell others about the president's dazzling speeches and the power he wielded. Yet in this relationship you would not really know him unless you got to spend time with him alone. Again, meaningful relationships are built only through communication.

In addition, you could not really trust the president without private conversation because outward behavior does not always reveal the heart. It is sad to say, again, that this type of relationship illustrates how many relate to God. These tell what they know about God and brag about His power, just as one would who traveled with the president, but they are still watching from the outside and do not truly know Him.

Listening is essential. Communication is a two-way street. God does not always need to hear our voices, for He already knows our thoughts and desires (1 Cor. 3:20; Matt. 9:4; Luke 16:15; Matt. 6:8). On the contrary, we need to hear His voice to have a close relationship, for we need to know His thoughts and His desires. Jesus said, "My sheep hear my voice, and I know them, and they follow me" (John 10:27). We create a real and productive relationship to God only through hearing His voice directly, and fulfilling our purpose in life begins with hearing His voice.

A most sobering reality is that if you do not hear His voice, you may not be His sheep. Jesus also said, "He that is of God heareth God's words: ye therefore hear them not, because ye are not of God" (John 8:47). We again should take heed at the strong words of our Lord.

In the same way that God wanted to marry Israel and be her Husband, He wants the same with us today.

The old covenant failed because men used it principally to change their outward behavior without inward conviction, which is hypocrisy. In fact, any covenant or relationship will fail unless Jesus is the Mediator. Though Moses had a great relationship with God, he failed as a mediator. He took no one into the promised land, not even himself. And of a whole generation that followed Moses, only Joshua and Caleb entered in, and that was because of their own faith in (relationship with) God, picturing the new covenant. No matter how close to God your leader, elder, or pastor is, he cannot get you into the promised land. Moses couldn't; Paul couldn't; only Jesus can.

Two Brothers: Two Trees

The two trees depicting two covenants also represent the two sons of Abraham: Ishmael and Isaac. Ishmael symbolizes the old covenant and the tree of the knowledge of good and evil, for he came through his mother, Hagar, and Paul said that "Agar" is Mount Sinai (Gal. 4:25). Hagar was an Egyptian, and her conception of Ishmael was from Abraham's own understanding and will, representing the tree of the knowledge of good and evil. Ishmael pictures the law, and as Ishmael came from Hagar, the law came from Mount Sinai (Gal. 4:22–25). Abraham was impatient and unwilling to wait for God to fulfill His promise in Isaac, so he had a child through Hagar.

In contrast, Isaac was the child of God's will and not Abraham or Sarah's, and he represents the tree of life, and the new covenant. In Genesis 22:18, God promised Abraham that "in thy seed shall all the nations of the earth be blessed," which referred to Jesus. Isaac, the seed of Abraham, is a picture of this promise, and a picture of the Lord Jesus (Heb. 11:17–19).

While Ishmael was the child of the flesh, Isaac was the child of the promise or the child of faith.

Isaac prefigured Jesus further when Abraham took Isaac to Mount Moriah to sacrifice him. Unknowingly, Isaac even carried the wood up the hill for the altar on his own back (Gen. 22:6). This parallels the Lord Jesus carrying the wooden cross of Calvary on His back up the hill to Golgotha, which means "skull."

It is interesting that the highest point on Mount Moriah is not the temple mound, but slightly north and outside the north wall of the city at a place where the rock ledge looks like a skull. (Today, it lies behind the Jerusalem bus station). This spot is right outside the garden wall, which some think is the location of the tomb in which Jesus was buried. This site not only gives the appearance of a skull, but it was also outside the city gate (Heb. 13:12). It appears that Jesus was sacrificed at the highest point on Mount Moriah.

Accordingly, I would assume that Abraham offered Issac at the highest point as well, and not at the site of the temple mound. In fact, I would imagine that these two events occurred in the exact same spot on Mount Moriah. I would not even be surprised if the wood that Isaac carried (possibly from Beersheba), and the cross that Jesus carried came from the same type of tree. And since many types of trees live more than two thousand years, maybe it was even the same tree. Nevertheless, this wood that Isaac carried up Mount Moriah, just like the cross that Jesus carried, symbolizes the tree of the knowledge of good and evil. This wood, as you may have already presumed, was most likely oak or cedar.

Two Brothers: Two Covenants

Because of Abraham's unbelief, Ishmael (Old Testament) came about before Isaac (New Testament). In the same way, because of the Israelites' unbelief at Mount Sinai, the bondage of the law of Moses (old covenant) came about before Christ (new covenant). Today, God blinds those who take His name (Christian) but do not want an intimate relationship, and He gives them the bondage of religious activities. Hebrews 3:19 says, "They could not enter in [God's rest] because of unbelief."

These two brothers further picture the two covenants in their provisions. When Abraham sent Ishmael and Hagar out into the desert, he gave them bread and water (Gen. 21:14). In the same way, God gave the Israelites who wandered in the wilderness (desert) bread (manna) and water (from the rock), for this is the old covenant of law. Bread and water alone picture mere sustenance, but no joy or flavor. This is probably why receiving only bread and water has always been a punishment or the diet of prisoners. Thus, it is what people in "bondage" (old covenant) would eat.

I suspect, however, that when Abraham gave Isaac a feast after he was weaned (Gen. 21:8), he served bread and wine just as Melchizedek served Abraham (Gen. 14:18). Remember that wine is the crushed fruit of the vine and bread is the crushed fruit of the grain (wheat). "Wine maketh merry" (Eccl. 10:19) and adds flavor to life. It represents those in the new covenant who are free to produce the fruit of the Spirit.

It is no coincidence that Jesus' first recorded miracle was changing water to wine (John 2). Jesus changed the old covenant of law into the new covenant of faith. This is why this miracle is so important. He changed the tree of the knowledge of good and evil to the tree of life. He changed Ishmael into Isaac. He changed flesh into Spirit and death into life—eternal life.

And Two Sisters

Now the tree of the knowledge of good and evil and the tree of life represent two spiritual states of man: death and life. They represent two covenants, old (law) and new (faith). They represent two types of trees, cedars or oaks and fruit-bearing trees. They represent two brothers, Ishmael and Isaac, and they also represent two sisters, Martha and Mary.

Martha, you'll remember, acted out of her own understanding and appeared constantly worried about the work to be done. She liked to judge others by her standard and decide what was fair. In contrast, Mary sought only a relationship with the Lord. She probably forgot anyone else was in the room when Jesus was present.

> Now it came to pass, as they went, that he
> entered into a certain village: and a certain
> woman named Martha received him into her
> house. And she had a sister called Mary, which

also sat at Jesus' feet, and heard his word.
But Martha was cumbered about much serving,
and came to him, and said, Lord, dost thou not
care that my sister hath left me to serve alone?
Bid her therefore that she help me. And Jesus
answered and said unto her, Martha, Martha,
thou art careful and troubled about many things:
But one thing is needful: and Mary hath chosen
that good part, which shall not be taken
away from her. (Luke 10:38–42)

When the Lord went to Martha's house, her sister just sat at Jesus' feet to hear His words. Mary chose the best "activity," which was to eat from the tree of life. Martha trusted in her own efforts and works instead of listening to the Lord. She somehow held this lie in her heart, that she had to *do* something, and this is what produced her anxiety and troubles. Martha was more worried about what Mary was not doing than about her own actions. Martha was eating from the good side of the tree of the knowledge of good and evil. Her working was certainly a good thing and not evil, but it still brought death. Her serving (works) would burn up in the fire of judgment.

But to many people, Martha was the better person, for she was industrious, hardworking, responsible, and outwardly she loved Jesus. These same people would see Mary as lazy, irresponsible, neglectful of her company, and even flippant. But the guests didn't come to eat, they came to hear Jesus. Martha, like so many today, are so busy trying to serve God, they don't spend time hearing His voice, and they don't really know Him. God desires our fellowship so much—but He does not need us or our efforts. We need Him. In the same way, I do not need my children, but I desire their fellowship and love more than any other earthly thing. Yet they do need me.

Mary's only understanding was that she needed Him, and Jesus said that would "not be taken away from her." Mary's focus on Jesus' person pleased Him, and she repeated her loving service to Him later: "It was that Mary which anointed the Lord with ointment, and wiped his feet with her hair" (John 11:2).

Martha: Practical but Unbelieving

In addition, Martha and Mary had a brother named Lazarus who became sick. The two sisters sent for the Lord, but Lazarus was dead four days before Jesus arrived.

> Then Martha, as soon as she heard that Jesus was coming, went and met him: but Mary sat still in the house. Then said Martha unto Jesus, Lord, if thou hadst been here, my brother had not died. But I know, that even now, whatsoever thou wilt ask of God, God will give it thee. Jesus saith unto her, Thy brother shall rise again. Martha saith unto him, I know that he shall rise again in the resurrection at the last day. Jesus said unto her,

> I am the resurrection, and the life: he that
> believeth in me, though he were dead, yet shall he
> live: And whosoever liveth and believeth in me
> shall never die. Believest thou this? She saith unto
> him, Yea, Lord: I believe that thou art the Christ,
> the Son of God, which should come into the
> world. And when she had so said, she went her
> way, and called Mary her sister secretly, saying,
> The Master is come, and calleth for thee. As soon
> as she heard that, she arose quickly, and came
> unto him. (John 11:20–29)

Mary trusted thoroughly in the Lord and sought only to spend time with Him, and she depicts the tree of life. Martha understood intellectually who Jesus was but did not totally trust in Him, for she trusted in her own understanding. This is evident in her need to warn Jesus of the odor from her brother's corpse:

> Jesus therefore again groaning in himself cometh
> to the grave. It was a cave, and a stone lay upon
> it. Jesus said, Take ye away the stone. Martha, the
> sister of him that was dead, saith unto him, Lord,
> by this time he stinketh: for he hath been dead
> four days. Jesus saith unto her, Said I not unto
> thee, that, if thou wouldest believe, thou
> shouldest see the glory of God? (John 11:38-40)

Martha was very practical in her own understanding, but she still expressed unbelief. Had she truly trusted Christ's words, she might have expected a restored (clean-smelling) Lazarus to walk from the cave. Any time we use our own understanding, we are telling God we know better. Martha told Jesus he was the Christ, the Son of God but then felt the need to warn him about the smell. This is being double minded as the Bible describes in James 1:6–8.

We must resemble fruit trees and not cedars. We must be of Isaac and not Ishmael. We must have Mary's heart and not Martha's. We must be of the covenant of faith and not of law. We must be born of the Spirit and not just flesh. We must be intimate with Jesus and not just behave well. We must have the tree of life planted in us to produce the fruit of the Spirit and fulfill the first commandment, "*Parah rabah.*"

Chapter 8
Religion: Beware the Snare

The tree of death, curse, and law yields solely the poison fruits of our flesh, while the fruit of the Spirit grows only on the tree of life; and this tree of life may also be called the tree of relationship. It is only through relationship that we produce fruit. Just as "the fruit of the womb" (children) are produced through the relationship or covenant of marriage, "the fruit of the Spirit" comes through relationship or covenant with Christ. This tree of relationship begins to grow in us when we receive the Seed of this tree (Jesus) and begin our relationship (covenant) with Christ.

If the tree of life is the tree of relationship, then what is the contrasting name for the tree of death? It is the tree of religion. Religion makes one look "good," like the tree of the knowledge of good and evil, but still brings death. *Religion is the outward behavior without an inward conversion of the soul; it is hypocrisy.* It is choosing "good" activities or behaviors based on our own understanding or definition of good. Those who practice religion rather than relationship tend to look down on those who do the opposite. Such people are eating from the good side of the tree of death, and they believe they have favor with God because compared to others, they are better at practicing what religion requires. Their works may make them feel comfortable and secure, but without faith they are still dead (Gal. 2:16).

As long as we use our own understanding, we are still on the wrong tree. Like Martha, we may choose works from the "good" side of this deceitful tree, but they still bring death. This is the tree of hypocrisy; this is the tree of religion.

God's View of Religion

God's viewpoint of religion might surprise you: He hates it. While the word *religion* is one our culture often considers a positive thing, the New Testament does not reflect this belief. The word "*religion*" (or "*religious*") occurs only five times in the New Testament translation we are using (King James Version). The first Greek word, *ioudaismos*, occurs twice (Gal. 1:13–14) and is translated "the Jews' religion" in both occurrences. Paul used this word meaning "Judaism," which merely represents the religion or ceremonial practice of the Jews.

The other three occurrences are in Acts 26:5 and James 1:26–27, in which the word "*religion*" is translated from the Greek word *threskeia*, meaning "ceremonial" or "outward behavior," or the external aspects of religious actions. More specifically, this Greek word translated as "religion" refers to the outward worship one does before men without necessarily an inward conviction.

Threskeia also occurs in Colossians 2:18 but is not translated as "religion." It is translated "worshipping," and in this verse it refers to the outward worship of angels (which Paul condemned). The Greek word *theosebeia*, which occurs in John 9:31, refers to the inward (known to God only) worship or reverence toward God; this term is never translated as "religion" in our Bibles. In no way do I wish to offend someone who holds to a good definition of the word *religion*, but in the New Testament, it has an air of outward behavior without inward reverence. This is hypocrisy.

Jesus' Take on Religion

In His teaching on the mount, Jesus shared what He felt about this outward behavior of men.

> And when thou prayest, thou shalt not be as the
> hypocrites are: for they love to pray standing in
> the synagogues and in the quarters of the streets,
> that they may be seen of men. Verily, I say unto
> you, They have their reward. But thou, when
> thou prayest, enter into thy closet, and when thou
> hast shut thy door, pray to thy Father which is in
> secret; and thy Father which seeth in secret shall
> reward thee openly. (Matthew 6:5–6)

Jesus loathed the outward behavior of *threskeia* yet praised inward or secret worship (*theosebeia*).

The Lord gave additional comments on hypocrisy:

> Ye hypocrites, well did Esaias prophesy of you,
> saying, This people draweth nigh unto me with
> their mouth, and honoureth me with their lips;
> but their heart is far from me. But in vain they do
> worship me [religious behavior], teaching for doc-
> trines the commandments of men. (Matt. 15:7–9)

Jesus' brother added another: "If any man among you seem to be religious, and bridleth not his tongue, but deceiveth his own heart, this man's religion [*threskeia*] is vain [worthless]" (James 1:26). No matter what our outward behavior, God looks at our hearts (Acts 1:24), and through the centuries so many have been deceived and believe they are born of God when they're not.

Now, can religion (*threskeia*) be good? The final occur-rence of the word is in James and is quite interesting, for it reads, "Pure religion and undefiled before God and the Father is this, To visit the fatherless and widows in their affliction, and to keep himself unspotted from the world" (1:27). Here we see mention of a "pure religion" or outward behavior. For the outward behavior to be pure, there must be a correspon-ding inward reverence or fear of God. This behavior would be "undefiled" and not hypocritical.

The Lord's brother James was using a play on words by saying that there are two outward behaviors that God approves. The first is providing the needs of orphans and widows. Scripture encourages this practice repeatedly (Matt. 19:21; Luke 14:13; Acts 20:35). The other behavior that apparently God approves is to keep ourselves separate or "unspotted from the world." This defines the word *holy*. "But as he which hath called you is holy, so be ye holy in all manner of conversation [behavior]; because it is written, Be ye holy; for I am holy" (1 Peter 1:15–16). God is separate from this worldly kingdom of Satan, and He expects His children to be separate also.

The practice of religion, except feeding widows and orphans and keeping ourselves separate from the ways of the world, is clearly something that God condemns. Caring for the poor and seeking to be pure: these are the only worthwhile religious acts in God's eyes, and that is because these actions arise from an inward respect for Him.

Beware the Snare

Once we have begun a relationship with God and receive the Seed from the tree of life, Satan sets a trap or snare to keep us from truly serving God: "Fear, and the pit, and the snare, shall be upon thee, O inhabitant of Moab, saith the LORD . . . He that getteth up out of the pit shall be taken in the snare" (Jer. 48:43–44).

The pit is the place we all are born into because of the curse of Adam; it is where we are held in the fear of death, awaiting God's judgment of our sin. The Old Testament lists more than one hundred references to what Psalm 55:23 calls "the pit of destruction." Repeatedly these ancient writers warned against going down into it. When we escape the pit we receive new life and see God's light (Job 33:28–30). When we receive the Seed of eternal life, we are freed from the pit, yet the snare is waiting for us.

The concept of the snare occurs more than eighty times in the Old Testament. God warned Israel specifically not to be snared by making covenant with any other nation (Ex. 34:12). Psalm 91:3, 124:7, and Ecclesiastes 9:12 refer to our being caught in the snare of the "fowler" or bird hunter, which represents Satan trying to tempt us with "bait." Actually, Hosea 9:8 says that this fowler uses a prophet (obviously a false one or wolf in sheep's clothing) as a snare. Unlike the bait the fowler uses for birds, Satan uses the things of this world.

Furthermore, Solomon warned us of the snare of friendship with evil or angry men (Prov. 22:24–25, 29:6). And Jesus said: "Take heed to yourselves, lest at any time your hearts be overcharged with surfeiting, and drunkenness, and cares of this life, and so that day come upon you unawares. For as a snare shall it come on all them that dwell on the face of the whole earth" (Luke 21:34–35). Satan will offer the snare to everyone who tries to serve God. Finally, Paul wrote Timothy of the "snare of the devil" and the dangers of falling into "temptation and a snare" (1 Tim. 3:7, 6:9).

The snare is religion: "The fear of man bringeth a snare: but whoso putteth his trust in the LORD shall be safe" (Prov.

29:25). Fear of man occurs when we worry about what others think of us. Yes, this often brings about good behavior, but it is bondage to men, and it is a trap. Desiring the approval of men comes from a fear of men, and this is religion. When we outwardly act pious toward God but inwardly desire to please or impress man, this is hypocrisy.

Fear is actually equal to faith. If we fear God, then we obviously have faith that He exists. There is no way to be intimate with God and not fear Him. It is not that you dread being close to Him, but you fear His judgments. It is this fear that breaks our proud, hard hearts to receive the Seed in repentance. This "fear of the LORD is the beginning of knowledge" (Prov. 1:7) and "the beginning of wisdom" (Prov. 9:10). It is through fear that we come to know Him and know Him better.

I have heard many say that this fear of God is more a "respect" or "awe," but this is a lie. Moses did not just respect God when he said, "I exceedingly fear and quake [shake violently]" (Heb. 12:21), or when he told the Israelites that they should have God's fear before their faces to keep them from sinning (Exod. 20:20). My greatest peace with God comes when I fear His judgments, and in fact, the closer I get to Him, the more I fear Him. Since faith is equal to fear, then the more I grow in fear, the more I grow in faith. Just as my children must fear my judgments (not me) to love me, to love God is to fear His judgments. It is wonderful, for "how unsearchable are his judgments, and his ways past finding out" (Rom. 11:33).

In the same way, the fear of man requires faith in man. When we worry how we appear to others (the way Martha did), then we are trusting in their opinions. Just as it is impossible to please God without faith, you cannot please men without relying upon them and their world. Just like the bramble we saw in Judges 9, men want you to "trust in [their] shadow[s]." They want you to fear and follow them, and this is religion.

Part of the trick, or rather the snare, is that deceivers may come in the name of Jesus. These "wolves" relate their doctrines and traditions and inspire the fear of men, which produces both pride and guilt, instead of teaching the fear of God that yields the fruits of humility and peace. As we've seen, Jesus said of such people, "In vain they do worship me, teaching for doctrines the commandments of men" (Matt. 15:9). Religious rules come from man's understandings of God's law, and the devil's snare is to get you to follow your own or other men's rules, believing they are from God. Many leaders are the prophets (wolves) that the fowler (Satan) uses to snare us with religion.

The snare of religion lies in our taking the law of God, twisting it in our own cursed understanding, blinding ourselves with pride as we think we fulfill it, and judging those who do not follow according to our understanding, tradition, lifestyle, and doctrine. Instead, we should judge ourselves with the law of God out of fear and humble ourselves toward others, which produces the fruit of the Spirit.

God's Law Plus Man's Ideas

Man has always rationalized and even added to God's law, beginning in the garden with Adam and Eve. God told Adam not to eat of the tree of the knowledge of good and evil, but when Eve recited the law to the serpent, she added, "neither shall ye touch it" (Gen. 3:3). God did not say they could not touch it. He just said they could not eat it.

Even more, the Pharisees and Scribes took the single commandment of the Sabbath and expanded it out of their own understanding into more than one thousand laws! Then they forced the people to keep them. This is bondage and it brings death. "My people are destroyed for lack of knowledge: because thou hast rejected knowledge, I will also reject thee, that thou shalt be no priest to me: seeing thou hast forgotten the law of thy God, I will also forget thy children" (Hos. 4:6).

The Jews thought they were following God, but they were heeding only the laws (understanding) of men. This lack of knowledge caused destruction in their lives because they did not hear God. To demonstrate this to the people, Jesus purposefully broke the Pharisees' laws right in front of them (for example, Luke 6:4–6), but He never broke God's law.

As an example of the extreme foolishness that man's laws can cause over time, we should examine the origin of the Jewish tradition regarding eating meat and dairy products together. The plethora of religious regulations that Jews have observed in this regard over the last two millennia have only one biblical reference: Exodus 23:19. This single verse simply instructs the Israelites not to boil a goat in its mother's milk. Somehow through "logic," Jewish scholars reasoned that these foods mingling in the human stomach was analogous to their being boiled together. Therefore eating the meat of a baby goat while consuming dairy products from its mother would be breaking God's law.

From this initial reasoning, years of tradition and further religiosity have exaggerated a small commandment into wealthy, modern-day Jews having two dishwashers in their kitchens: one to wash their dairy plates, one to wash their meat plates.

These layers of man-made laws that surround the original commandment are sometimes called "fence laws," as they protect one from breaking the original commandment contained inside. A twenty-first-century example of this would be to post speed-limit signs of thirty miles per hour even though the true speed limit is fifty-five. This would help keep people from breaking the real law. Yes, some would break the law of thirty miles per hour, but few would push the pedal enough to exceed the original fifty-five-miles-per-hour law.

These examples picture how people might try to intercede in others' relationships with God. When we do this, we demonstrate that we do not trust God to handle His relationships with others, that we believe He needs us to judge them and keep them in line. We are actually deceiving people, telling them we are correcting them for their own good. Even if they keep our additions to the law, they are not hearing God directly and we become their mediator. Therefore, they again are under the old covenant and do not have a close relationship with God. This is religion.

Man's Rules Versus God's

Different denominations, movements, organizations, and churches have developed rules based on their own understanding, and their members unknowingly follow them, thinking they are obeying God. But actually they are just obeying men. They often judge others (as the Pharisees did Jesus) who do not heed "their" rules. These unknowing followers believe they know God because they know their church doctrine or culture. This belief causes the same division that existed between the Pharisees and Sadducees. This is religion; it brings death.

Walking in the Spirit would produce unity in the true body of Christ because we would all follow one Spirit instead of many traditions. We are to be one as Jesus and the Father are one (John 17:21). Jesus is returning not for a harem but a single, faithful bride. There should only be one will, which is that of the Father.

Many so-called Christians say they trust God, but their actions show they trust in their own understanding. We desire our own children to trust in our rules and our desires at all times and not act on their own understanding. Why would God want His children to be any different? We must remove ourselves from this tree of the knowledge of good and evil. We must avoid this double-minded religious bondage of hypocrisy, which is a snare.

There were two trees in the garden, symbolizing life and death. Only the tree of life fulfilled its purpose in creation by yielding the fruit of the Spirit and multiplying. The tree of death brought a curse to all men, and this tree became the cross on which Jesus died. The Lord's death and resurrection brought a cure to humanity, but only to those who believe. While in Old Testament times these two trees may have been known as the trees of law and faith, today under the new covenant they are more aptly called the tree of religion and the tree of relationship with Christ.

The good fruit from the tree of relationship is good throughout, while the poison fruit from the tree of religion is deceitful and good only on the outside, just like the religious person. Yet God looks at and judges the inside of both the person as well as the fruit. We should take heed and seek ever more passionately to fulfill His first commandment, "Be fruitful, and multiply."

Chapter 9
Planting the Seed

We have seen how we begin to fulfill the first commandment when the Seed of the tree of life, namely Jesus, is planted in our hearts. From this spiritual Seed we may grow and bear the fruit (be fruitful) of the Spirit. From this fruit God harvests seed that can be sowed or planted in others' hearts (and multiply). In this chapter, let us examine the ways the initial planting begins our relationship with God.

In John 12:24 Jesus said, "Verily, verily, I say unto you, Except a corn of wheat fall into the ground and die, it abideth alone: but if it die, it bringeth forth much fruit." Therefore, *when we receive Jesus into our hearts it is as spiritual seed into spiritual soil.* Jesus is the grain of wheat that died and now bears much fruit through multiplying. He planted the seed, which came from the spiritual fruit He produced in those who received Him while He was on earth after the resurrection. Those first new plants were the many disciples who followed Him, such as Peter, Paul, Mary Magdalene, and Nicodemus.

Again, Jesus was that original grain of wheat, and now He "bringeth forth much fruit" in us. All the true Christians of the past two thousand years who had or have the tree of life planted in them came from that single grain. The increase in number is the process of yield from the parable of the sower and fulfillment of the first commandment. It is the same Seed today as it was in the first century for Philip or Stephen, for God does not change, and neither does His spiritual seed. In fact, even millennia-old wheat seed recovered in archaeological digs shows little change.

A Secret Ceremony

Just as the sower placing the seed in the soil is a picture of the beginning of our relationship or covenant with Christ, so is the husband placing his seed in the bride the beginning of the relationship or covenant of marriage. This is why the Bible pictures us as the bride of Christ and Christ as the Bridegroom. As Christ (our Husband) places His spiritual seed in us, His bride, we begin this marriage covenant with Him.

God created this physical union between a man and his wife to illustrate the connection between Christ and His bride, in which "the two shall become one flesh." Humans, unlike animals, reproduce face-to-face, just as we are to meet the Lord Jesus "face-to-face." Just as the wife receives the seed from the husband to produce the fruit of the womb, we receive the Seed from our Husband, the Lord Jesus, to produce the fruit of the Spirit. In fact, the common Greek word for sowing or seed is *spermatoa*, the same word for the male human seed. It is through this union that conception occurs, and the Seed of the tree of life is planted in the new child of God so that he may fulfill the first commandment.

It is not the ceremony at the church that makes a couple married; it is the physical act of this union. In Genesis 24:67 we see: "Isaac brought [Rebekah] into his mother Sarah's tent, and took Rebekah, and she became his wife; and he loved her." Isaac and Rebekah had no ceremony; they had only a covenant and an intimacy between them.

The covenant of marriage begins when the husband places the seed in his bride, and it is the same way in our union with Christ. It is not the decision made before men in an assembly, but it is the private and secret union that a husband and wife share that creates their bond. Jesus recognized marriage by the act of intimacy.

For example, look at the Lord's response to the woman at the well when she told Him she had no husband. "Thou hast well said, I have no husband: For thou hast had five husbands; and he whom thou now hast is not thy husband: in that saidst thou truly" (John 4:17–18). The woman had several "husbands" in that she had been intimate with several men, but the current man she was with was married to someone else. The Samarian culture of that era would not have tolerated five ceremonies for this woman without stoning her. Therefore, Jesus recognized these five men as husbands because the woman had had private union with them.

We have our own "private union" with Christ our Husband through personal and private time we spend alone with Him. The intimate bond between a husband and wife is just like the one we, the bride, share with Christ the Bridegroom. Paul referred to this, saying, "This is a great mystery: but I speak concerning Christ and the church" (Eph. 5:32). The word translated "mystery" is the Greek word *musterion*, which simply means "hidden" or "secret." Just as there is intimate knowledge that husbands and wives share only between themselves, there are secrets that Christ shares only with His bride (those who are intimate with Him).

Even on earth, Jesus did not share His secrets with everyone. "And he said unto [the Twelve], Unto you it is given to know the mystery of the kingdom of God: but unto them that are without, all these things are done in parables: That seeing they may see, and not perceive; and hearing they may hear, and not understand" (Mark 4:11–12). Jesus would reveal His mysteries only to those close to Him.

A farmer plants seed in the ground in hopes of yielding fruit, just as the husband plants the seed in the wife in hopes of producing the fruit of the womb. In the same way, Christ plants His seed in us so that we will produce the fruit of the Spirit. The seed is placed in the covenant of marriage when the couple spends time alone in relationship. This is true for husbands and wives, and for Christ and His church. *Just as the husband desires intimacy with his wife, Christ desires an intimate relationship with us.*

The Intimacy He Desires

I know thousands of people, and many I know well; but I know only one intimately: my bride. The intensely personal aspect of this relationship is contained in a Greek word often translated "know" in the New Testament: *ginosko.*

This word is a great help in understanding the intimate relationship with Christ. Several Greek words mean "knowledge" or "knowing," but the principle two are *ginosko* and *oida. Oida* usually represents knowledge that is intuitive and does not necessarily come from experience. Ginosko is knowledge through experience. First Corinthians 2:12–14 says:

> Now we have received, not the spirit of the
> world, but the Spirit which is of God; that we
> might know [*oida*] the things that are freely
> given to us of God. Which things also we speak,
> not in the words which man's wisdom teacheth,
> but which the Holy Ghost teacheth; comparing
> spiritual things with spiritual. But the natural
> man receiveth not the things of the Spirit of
> God: for they are foolishness unto him: neither
> can he know [*ginosko*] them, because they are
> spiritually discerned.

We see first that *oida* is knowledge "that [is] freely given to us of God." No experience is involved with *oida*; the Spirit of God reveals these things.

In verse 14 we see that the "natural man" cannot know (*ginosko*) or discern things of God because they are spiritual. The natural man has no experience in a relationship with God and has therefore no knowledge through experience.

Knowledge from experience is very important. You can trust someone based only on the experience you have with him. Bad experiences may demonstrate that someone is untrustworthy, while good experiences may prove otherwise. The more we trust someone, the more we will see whether he is truly faithful and deserving of our trust.

As an aside, many who think they have found God to be untrustworthy carry hurt or bitterness toward Him. They should direct their anger not at God, but at their own flesh. God is always faithful and trustworthy, and these people were not trusting in God but in their own understanding. They had put God in some box based on their doctrine, tradition, or theology. They were hurt because they loved something more than God. Since they were not seeking His will, they were disappointed, and they blamed God for their letdown. They lacked *ginosko*.

Experience Plus Intimacy

Ginosko knowledge is not just experiential, but it is intimate just as the husband is with his wife. In Luke 1:26–33, the angel Gabriel appeared to Mary and told her that she would have a child. In verse 34, Mary asked, "How shall this be, seeing I know not a man?" The Greek word here for "know" is *ginosko* again. Mary knew many men, and she was actually betrothed or engaged to Joseph, but she did not "know" any man intimately. Modern translations will say that Mary "was a virgin," which is true but not an accurate rendering from the Greek. They lose the meaning of *ginosko* being intimate knowledge.

In Matthew 1:20–24, the angel of the Lord informed Joseph that his betrothed, Mary, was pregnant with the Lord Jesus, and that she should remain a virgin according to modern translations until His delivery. Verse 25 says, "And [Joseph] knew her not till she had brought forth her firstborn son: and he called his name JESUS." Obviously, Joseph knew Mary and knew her very well. Remember how Joseph led the pregnant Mary on a donkey to Bethlehem? But again, he did not "know" her intimately. The Greek word here is *ginosko*. Just as *ginosko* means experience, Mary and Joseph had no intimate experience, and Mary remained a virgin until after Jesus was born. Again, modern translations miss this.

This same picture exists in the Hebrew language. Genesis 4:1 says, "Adam knew Eve his wife; and she conceived, and bare Cain." Later in verse 17, "Cain knew his wife; and she conceived, and bare Enoch." Obviously this intimate knowledge produced a conception. In the same way, John 17:3 says, "This is life eternal, that they may know [*ginosko*] thee the only true God." This knowledge is an intimate relationship, and it is this intimate relationship with the Lord Jesus that is eternal life. It is through this relationship or covenant that the Seed of eternal life (tree of life) is planted in us.

Intimate Knowledge

In our culture, a woman leaves her family and as a wife, joins that of her husband, becoming part of him. In the same way we leave the family of this world when we are born again and become part of the family of God through our Husband, the Lord Jesus. A wife is "set free" from her previous family or "seed," to join the family or "seed" of her husband.

In the same way, we are set free from the tree of the knowledge of good and evil (our earthly family or seed from Adam), and the Seed of the tree of life (our Husband's seed) is planted in us. "Ye shall know [*ginosko*] the truth, and the truth shall make you free" (John 8:32). Again it is *ginosko*, this intimate knowledge and experience that sets us free from the curse, death, law, flesh, and religion.

Just as the two become one flesh, we are joined to Christ as His bride, and we must be careful not to be as the "silly women" in Ephesus who were "ever learning, and never able to come to the knowledge [*ginosko*] of the truth" (2 Tim. 3:6–7). These women sought and learned information but never abided in the intimate knowledge that comes from experience. They remained separate from the Husband (Christ) and still joined to the world.

Again, Matthew 7:22–23 says, "Many will say to me in that day, Lord, Lord, have we not prophesied in thy name? And in thy name have cast out devils? And in thy name done many wonderful works? And then will I profess unto them, I never knew [*ginosko*] you: depart from me, ye that work iniquity." These individuals did many great works and signs but they never had this intimate relationship or knowledge (*ginosko*) through experience with the Lord Jesus, and they were cast out into outer darkness.

What is this intimate knowledge or relationship with Jesus that the deceivers and the "silly women" did not posses? What is this relationship signified by *ginosko*? It is eternal life. Look again at John 17:3 where Jesus defined eternal life (or having the eternal tree of life planted in us): "This is life eternal, that they might know (*ginosko*) thee the only true God, and Jesus Christ, whom thou hast sent."

Eternal life begins in this physical life when we receive the eternal Seed from the eternal tree, who is our Husband, the Lord Jesus. Eternal life is simply knowing God intimately, and this comes only from spending time alone with Him. Eternal life comes from an intimate relationship with God that is personal and private, and this is just like the mysterious and confidential relationship between a husband and his bride. This is why the Bible pictures us as the bride of Christ, and He is the Bridegroom.

Love and Friendship

Just as you would not marry anyone whom you did not love more than anyone else, you would not have a close friendship with anyone you did not greatly love. We see this in the use of the word "*friend*" in the Old Testament. The word "*friend*" in English Bibles is usually translated from the Hebrew word *rea*, which refers to someone who may be an associate or a companion. But four times the word *friend* is translated from *ahab*, which involves an affection that is even more intimate.

Second Chronicles 20:7 says, "Art thou not our God, who didst drive out the inhabitants of this land before thy people Israel, and gavest it to the seed of Abraham thy friend [*ahab*] for ever?" Abraham was an intimate friend of God, and this word suggests great affection between them. And again: "But thou, Israel, art my servant, Jacob whom I have chosen, the seed of Abraham my friend [*ahab*]" (Isa. 41:8). Abraham was obviously more than a companion or an associate of God.

Proverbs 18:24 says, "A man that hath friends must show himself friendly: and there is a friend that sticketh closer than a brother." This verse is very interesting. The word "friends" in this verse is *rea*, meaning " a companion or associate," and to these we must be "friendly." But this "friend that sticketh closer than a brother" is *ahab* and represents the relationship between Abraham and God. This relationship involves an intimacy that is deeper than you would have with your own brother.

Proverbs 27:6 says, "Faithful are the wounds of a friend; but the kisses of an enemy are deceitful." Again, the word "friend" is *ahab*, meaning someone very close to us. As the Lord Jesus through the Holy Spirit reveals to us our weaknesses and prunes out the bad part of our branches, it hurts, and we are often wounded. But He is faithful, and He points out our weaknesses from love and not self-promotion. It is a rare and intimate friend who can do this. Often only a spouse can suggest these kinds of corrections and keep the relationship. Abraham had this kind of relationship with God, and this is the intimate Friend we have in Jesus.

The beginning of this intimate relationship or covenant is receiving Jesus (the Seed) into our hearts. We see it pictured in Scripture, as well as in nature, as seed entering the soil and the husband placing his seed in the wife. This is a special relationship in which two share secrets, as the Greek word *ginosko* describes. From such a relationship comes fruit, and by it we fulfill the first commandment.

Chapter 10
Two Parts of the Seed

We saw in the last chapter the planting of the Seed, Jesus: "Except a corn of wheat fall into the ground and die, it abideth alone: but if it die, it bringeth forth much fruit" (John 12:24). This grain of wheat that enters the earth pictures Jesus' burial (planting), and He is the Seed that replanted the tree of life. As God kept Adam from the tree of life after the Fall (Gen. 3), He replanted this tree in the burial of Christ, and the seed from His fruit can be planted in us.

In this chapter we will see that there are two parts of a seed, and these represent two parts of the sacrifice (death and burial) of Christ. Most all seeds have two parts. First, there is the *embryo* that develops into the new plant. This is the part of the seed that carries "the life" to the developing plant. The embryo determines what kind of plant will grow from the seed, and what kind of fruit the plant will produce. As the embryo begins to grow, this is called germination.

The other part of the seed is the *endosperm* or the fleshy part of the seed. The endosperm contains stored energy in the form of starch that sustains the new plant until it reaches sunlight and begins photosynthesis. This starch requires oxygen to generate energy—this is why seeds need oxygen in the soil to germinate. But once these seeds become plants their metabolism changes, and they produce oxygen themselves.

As the embryo grows, it consumes the fleshy part until it is gone and the embryo produces a new plant. In fact, you usually plant a seed at a depth dependent on the size of the seed. Larger seeds with greater endosperm can usually be planted deeper because they have more stored energy to reach the surface. A seed planted too deep for its size will run out of energy before it reaches the surface and die.

The endosperm withers as the new plant climbs to the surface, or rather, the "flesh" must be destroyed for the embryo to give "life." Jesus and Paul affirmed this: "If it die, it bringeth forth much fruit" (John 12:24). "That which thou sowest is not quickened [made alive], except it die" (1 Cor. 15:36). This flesh (or endosperm) must die for the seed to grow.

Two Parts of Seed and Sacrifice

Just as there are two parts of a seed, there are two parts of the sacrifice of Christ.

Just as Adam was flesh and blood when he received the curse in the garden, God took on flesh and blood to take our curse away. The *logos* (Word) of God existed with God and was God, and then became flesh and dwelt among us (John 1:1,14) in the Person of Jesus Christ. Jesus partook of two parts (flesh and blood) just as we do. "As the children are partakers of flesh and blood, he also himself likewise took part of the same" (Heb. 2:14).

When Jesus died, His flesh was crucified, but His blood was "poured out" by a spear. He was made of flesh and blood, and these are the two parts of His sacrifice. These are also the two parts of the new covenant and the Lord's Supper (bread and wine).

Furthermore, the old covenant pictured these in the two parts of the Passover lamb (Exod. 12). First, there was the "fleshy" part of the lamb that the Israelites had to consume totally (either by eating it or burning it).

> Your lamb shall be without blemish, a male of the first year . . . And they shall eat the flesh in that night, roast with fire, and unleavened bread . . . And ye shall let nothing of it remain until the morning; and that which remaineth of it until the morning ye shall burn with fire . . . It is the LORD's Passover . . . And the blood shall be to you for a token upon the houses where ye are: and when I see the blood, I will pass over you, and the plague shall not be upon you to destroy you, when I smite the land of Egypt. And this

day shall be unto you for a memorial . . . ye shall
keep it a feast by an ordinance for ever. (Exodus
12:5,8,10,11,13–14)

Before the Lord visited the land of Egypt and passed over
the houses marked with blood, the Israelites had to consume
the flesh of the lamb. So the flesh must be destroyed before
God will look at the blood.

God is always consistent. If the fleshy part of the seed
must die for the embryo to give life, and Jesus' flesh had to be
crucified before the atonement, then the blood must give
(eternal) life: "For the life of the flesh is in the blood: and I
have given it to you upon the altar to make an atonement for
your souls: for it is the blood that maketh an atonement for
the soul" (Lev. 17:11). It is the blood of Jesus that gives us
eternal life and begins to grow as the eternal tree of life in us.

As we see repeatedly, destruction of the flesh (death) precedes the covenant in His blood (life). There must be death
before life, and in the same way, we partake of the bread (His
body) before the wine (His blood) in the Lord's Supper.
When we partake of the Lord's Supper, we are keeping the
Passover feast forever and ever, as He commanded. We are
renewing the covenant again and again.

The Blood of Christ

What is the most valuable commodity in all of history? It is
the blood of Christ Jesus. It paid the debt for all the disobedi-

ence and evil every person ever thought or did. But only those who trust in the promise of this precious blood can experience its cleansing. Abel's blood sacrifice before the Lord cleansed only him, not Cain. The sin offering of Leviticus 16 cleansed only the Israelites who trusted in the promise God gave Moses. The Israelites' offering in the tabernacle did not cleanse people from other nations.

Only those who trust in the promise of God are justified by the sacrifice: "The just shall live by faith" (Rom. 1:17; Gal. 3:11; Heb. 10:38). It was the same with Abel, Noah, Abraham, Moses, David, and it is the same with us today. Only those who trust (have faith) in the promise of God concerning the blood of His Son experience His cleansing.

As an example, consider our United States currency. Each bill has a number on it that you believe to declare its value, and the bill has value only because you and others trust (have faith) in it. The U.S. government guarantees its currency, and we must place faith in the promise of our government to benefit from the value of the bill. In fact, these bills (paper money) are sometimes called notes because that is short for "bank note" or "promissory note." We must trust in the promise behind the note, or better, trust in the one promising.

You would probably feel uncomfortable accepting currency from another government. Those foreign bills have a similar promise on them, but the one promising is different. Your concern with the currency is that you do not trust the foreign government as much as you do your own. It is the same with God, for when we do not believe the promises of God, it is because we do not believe in the one promising (God). Just as currency is valuable only to those who trust in its value, *the blood of Christ is valuable only to those who trust in it.*

The blood of Christ is precious only if you believe in God's promise: "Forasmuch as ye know that ye were not redeemed with corruptible things, as silver and gold [U.S. currency] . . . But with the precious blood of Christ, as of a lamb without blemish and without spot" (1 Peter 1:18–19). Gold and silver cannot be eaten in famine and will not rescue you from what is to come: "Their silver and their gold shall not be able to deliver them in the day of the wrath of the Lord: they shall not satisfy their souls, neither fill their bowels [as food]: because it is the stumblingblock of their iniquity" (Ezek. 17:19).

When wrath comes, you will no longer trust in silver and gold, and therefore they will have no value. God comes not to seek gold or silver but blood. Do you trust in the promises of God concerning the blood of the Lord Jesus? "Being justified freely by his grace through the redemption that is in Christ Jesus: Whom God hath set forth to be a propitiation through faith in his blood, to declare his righteousness for the remission of sins that are past, through the forbearance of God" (Rom. 3:24–25). Do you trust in His blood? Better yet, do you trust in the One promising?

Only this precious blood of the Lord Jesus can pay our debt for transgressing the law of God. Only this precious blood can give us life—eternal life. As the blood of the lamb or goat on the altar on earth temporarily made atonement for the sin of those who trusted in the promise, the blood of Jesus on the altar in heaven forever atones for the sin of those who trust in God's promise. Those who believe in "limited atonement" are correct: atonement is limited to those who trust in the promise concerning His blood.

The Body of Christ

Now we have briefly considered the blood of Christ represented by the wine in the Lord's Supper (1 Cor. 11:25) and the blood of the Passover lamb, but we must also consider the body of Christ represented by the bread in the Lord's Supper (1 Cor. 11:24) and body of the Passover lamb in the old covenant. You may ask, If the blood of Christ cleanses us from all sin, then what is the purpose of the body? Why must the flesh be destroyed first?

Let me answer this question by analogy. Suppose I had a son who was a thief, and he continually went around stealing at his will. As a father, I am responsible for my son's debts, but what can I do? If I had the means, I could go behind my son and pay for everything he stole. I could "make atonement" for all his crime and suffer the punishment of his errors, and my son would be free from his crime. But he would not be free from his curse—he would still be a thief. I may have covered his outward behavior with money, but inside he is still a criminal. He will go on and sin again, and there will not be any slowing of his stealing.

It would do me little good as a father to pay the debts of a thieving son unless he is dead (or cured). Once he is dead (or cured), I can cover the debt without worry of further debt. Therefore, it is only after our flesh is crucified with Christ (Gal. 2:20; Rom. 6:6) that the blood of Christ can atone for our sin (debt).

Now in the Lord's Supper the bread (Christ's body broken for us) always precedes the wine (His blood that was poured out for us). Jesus explained in Luke 22 as He served the Passover meal to His disciples that those elements were actually His body (flesh) and His blood. This is why the Passover lamb's flesh had to be consumed (eaten or burned) totally before God would see the blood. In the same way, the death of Christ on the cross precedes the spear piercing His side to release the blood and water. This order is no coincidence.

In the same way, while the blood of Christ makes atonement for our disobedience to God's law (in this case, "Thou shall not steal"), it is the body (flesh) of Christ that frees us from the curse (that makes my son a thief).

We must also be free from the curse of Adam to have a relationship with God. It is the Cross that frees us from the curse and restores our relationship to God. It is only through the body of Christ that we may enter into the Holy of Holies. When Christ died, immediately the veil of temple was torn from the top to the bottom (signifying God did it), creating access for all men to God through Christ by faith. This veil represented Christ's flesh (Heb. 10:20). We proceed unto the Holy of Holies through the Cross of Christ: "Let us therefore come boldly unto the throne of grace, that we may obtain mercy, and find grace to help in time of need" (Heb. 4:16).

We must pass through the veil (His body) before we receive the blood. We must be crucified before we receive atonement. We must deal with the sinner before we deal with the sin. We must deal with the thief before we deal with the stealing. We must enter into death (the Cross) before we receive life (the blood). Once our flesh is crucified with Christ's as we deny our souls, then the blood can give us life.

The two parts of the seed represent the two parts of Christ's sacrifice for us. Death must always precede life. Again, the Seed is the source of life, and the source of our being able to obey the first commandment.

Chapter 11
The Seed Must Die

We have seen that we receive the tree of life when the Seed of this tree is planted in us, and the planting of this Seed is the beginning of our relationship or covenant with Jesus. This seed has two parts. First, there is the "fleshy part" that must die, and this represents the crucified body of Christ. This flesh was hung on a cross (tree), thus breaking the curse from Adam eating from the wrong tree in the garden. Second, the embryo that carries the life represents the blood that was poured out, thus providing atonement for sin and instilling eternal life.

These two parts of the seed and these two parts of the sacrifice of Christ are subsequently buried (or planted). In three days this planting brings forth a glorious new plant (the Resurrection). This is the tree of life returned to man, and when we receive Jesus (Seed), this tree begins to grow in us as evidenced by the fruits of the Spirit. This may sound wonderful, but how does this seed germinate within us?

Look again at John 12:24 as well as verse 25: "Except a corn of wheat fall into the ground and die, it abideth alone: but if it die, it bringeth forth much fruit. He that loveth his life shall lose it; and he that hateth his life in this world shall keep it unto life eternal." We have seen that Jesus is the grain of wheat that dies, but verse 25 is clearly speaking of us. Do we die also as He died? Since dying leads us to eternal life and hating our lives leads us there as well, then could hating our lives represent the death that is required?

The kingdom of God is always the opposite of the world and our understanding, and it is opposed to the desires of our flesh and our fear of death, which keeps us in bondage to Satan (Heb. 2:15). Our flesh or soul, tell us that we must continue to live at all costs, *but in the kingdom of God, we must die to have life, and the beginning of eternal life is death* (hating our lives). Learning to live in the kingdom of God is learning to die to this world.

Losing Life to Save It

The next verse we are going to look at is very similar to what we saw in John 12:25: "Whosoever will save his life shall lose it; but whosoever shall lose his life for my sake and the gospel's, the same shall save it." The kingdom of God is so opposed to the kingdoms of this world that we must lose our lives in order to save them. This is hard to comprehend.

Revelation 12:11 says, "They overcame [Satan] by the blood of the Lamb, and by the word of their testimony; and they loved not their lives unto the death." We overcome the works and the power of Satan by hating our lives to the point of death: hating who we are in the flesh and rejecting those sinful behaviors. This is how we have victory over the world. This is how we receive eternal life and are born again of the Spirit. This is how we begin this new covenant, and the Seed begins to grow.

How can this be? Do we actually need to kill ourselves? Do we need a friend to nail us to a cross until we suffer death? Should we commit suicide? Because of our bondage to Satan and the fear of death, we tend to think of the physical existence as supreme. *It is not the physical life that is the enemy of God, but the soul, which wants to trust in its own understanding and be its own judge.*

Your soul is made up of your mind, emotions, desires, and will. God is not angry with your body but your soul, which is in rebellion to Him. The death of the soul and new birth of the Spirit have nothing to do with your physical body initially. We must not try to understand this in the physical realm. The kingdom of God is spiritual.

In John 3:1–10 a man had the problem of focusing on the physical realm.

> There was a man of the Pharisees, named
> Nicodemus, a ruler of the Jews: The same came
> to Jesus by night, and said unto him, Rabbi, we
> know that thou art a teacher come from God: for

no man can do these miracles that thou doest, except God be with him. Jesus answered and said unto him, Verily, verily, I say unto thee, Except a man be born again, he cannot see the kingdom of God. Nicodemus saith unto him, How can a man be born when he is old? Can he enter the second time into his mother's womb, and be born? Jesus answered, Verily, verily, I say unto thee, Except a man be born of water and of the Spirit, he cannot enter into the kingdom of God. That which is born of the flesh is flesh; and that which is born of the Spirit is spirit. Marvel not that I said unto thee, Ye must be born again. The wind bloweth were it listeth, and thou hearest the sound thereof, but canst not tell whence it cometh, and whither it goeth: so is every one that is born of the Spirit. Nicodemus answered and said unto him, How can these things be?

As Jesus was trying to relate the truth of the kingdom of God, Nicodemus was trying to understand how he could enter again into his mother's womb. This is the same as our wondering whether we should commit suicide in order to enter the kingdom of God.

If Nicodemus had again entered into his mother's womb and been born a second time, he still would have been born of the flesh! Jesus made this clear when he said, "That which is born of flesh is flesh." But what Nicodemus needed was a different birth, which was that of the Spirit. In the same way, if we died physically and were resurrected physically, then we would still have our cursed flesh and souls that are in rebellion to God. It is our souls that must die (be denied).

This concept of dying (denying our souls or hating our lives) is quite difficult to comprehend. A major problem is that we do not want to hear this! Our flesh or souls do not want to die (or be denied). It is so much easier to participate in some act of ministry or worship—some religious activity. These acts do not hurt. They do not require humility. Furthermore, the forces of darkness are always present, providing lies and twisted truth to hide the need for us to die. They offer us excuses and extensive rationalization so that we avoid dying to ourselves.

Many who call themselves Christian today are confused about this issue, but "God is not the author of confusion" (1 Cor. 14:33). It comes from the enemy. Satan holds the whole world in bondage, and the only way to escape it is to deny our souls and be crucified with Jesus. We die with Jesus by denying ourselves. In other words, we escape death by dying.

Psuche

Lucifer will go to any length to keep you from denying your soul and dying to sin. Part of our lack of clarity comes from our Bible translations. Some of our translators must have had the same problem that Nicodemus had in that they focused on the physical, and this caused them to change the translation of a particular word. For example, the Greek word *psuche* occurs approximately one hundred times in the New Testament writings. About seventy times it is translated "soul," and it is from this Greek word *psuche* that we get our word *psychology*. Psychology is the study of the soul.

Approximately thirty times the Greek word *psuche* is translated "life." Almost all of these occur in the four Gospels. If you were to examine each of these instances you would see they are referring to the laying down, "hating," or giving up of one's life. This is the problem. The translators were thinking in the physical realm, and therefore they felt that we had to die or give up our "lives" physically. But the gospel writers had no such intention.

If Matthew, Mark, Luke, and John had meant "life," they would have used the Greek word *zoe*. But they used *psuche*, which should be translated "soul." It's clear that the translation in Mark 8:34, for example, of "life" should be "soul" from the verses that follow it. Mark 8:34–37 says:

> Whosoever will come after me, let him deny
> himself, and take up his cross, and follow me.
> For whosoever will save his life [*psuche*] shall lose
> it; but whosoever shall lose his life [*psuche*] for
> my sake and the gospel's, the same shall save it.
> For what shall it profit a man, if he shall gain

the whole world, and lose his own soul? Or what
shall a man give in exchange for his soul? [*psuche*]

We must lose or lay down *our souls* in order to receive
Christ's eternal life. Many believe that denying themselves or
hating their lives means simply giving up money, possessions, or the things of this world. But those are all external
things and are not necessarily in rebellion to God. This
rejection or denial is an inward process in which we must
reject our desires or lusts after these things. Remember, sin is
the inward thought before the external action. It is our
thinking we need these things instead of needing God and
trusting Him to provide.

In addition, our most prized possessions are not external
but rather internal. They are our knowledge, our understanding, our doctrines, and our traditions; even more, they
are our opinions. Even more than these is the right we
believe we have to give an opinion. It is this desire to be
served instead of serving. It is this desire to please men and
receive honor. It is even the desire to have good character
and morals. We must reject all of these, for they all generate
independence from God.

We must crucify all of this, for it was traditions, doctrines, and opinions of men that crucified Christ. We must
learn to hate our old selves. We must learn to hate our foolishness. God wants us to focus on *our* sin, and *our* problems.
The religious person likes to focus on others' sin and general

sin, such as homosexuality, adultery, stealing, and murder, so that he doesn't have to deal with his inward sins of selfishness, bitterness, greed, and fear of man. We were born physically with a will that wants to impress God and look good before men instead of dying.

William Tyndale, the sole translator of the English Bible, wrote before he was imprisoned and then martyred that it's through suffering and persecution that God slowly crucifies and destroys our flesh. Tyndale wrote in 1528:

> Neverthelater He suffereth us to fall into many temptations and much adversity: yea, Himself layeth the cross of tribulation on our backs, not that He rejoiceth in our sorrow, but to drive sin out of the flesh, which can none otherwise be cured: as a physician and surgeon do many things that are painful to the sick, not that they rejoice in the pains of the poor wretches, but to persecute and drive out the diseases which can no otherwise be healed. (William Tyndale, *The Obedience of a Christian Man* [Columbus, Ohio: Lazareth Ministry Press, 1999], 231)

Pain helps alleviate our sin burden. And the more sufferings and rejections by men we endure, the more God's Spirit is free to grow within us. This is the life to which He calls us. This is why Jesus said, "Narrow is the way, which leadeth unto life, and few there be that find it" (Matt. 7:14).

This is how we become a "living" sacrifice: we sacrifice our desires, our flesh, our passions, and our will. In Mark 8:34, Jesus said we must deny ourselves and be crucified with Him. We do this as we deny our souls.

Living and Dying at the Same Time

Paul understood this. He wrote, "I am crucified with Christ: nevertheless I live; yet not I, but Christ liveth in me: and the life which I now live in the flesh I live by the faith of the Son of God, who loved me, and gave himself for me" (Gal. 2:20). How can this be? How could Paul be crucified with Christ yet still live to write his letters to us? How can we die and yet still live?

A concept from Romans 12:1–2 explains this living death. Paul said, "I beseech you therefore, brethren, by the mercies of God, that ye present your bodies a living sacrifice, holy, acceptable unto God, which is your reasonable service. And be not conformed to this world: but be ye transformed by the renewing of your mind, that ye may prove what is that good, and acceptable, and perfect, will of God." God's will is that we present ourselves as "living sacrifices," which prevents us from being conformed to the current world and transforms us to eternal life in Christ Jesus. The Greek word for "sacrifice" speaks of the killing of flesh or can refer to that which is sacrificed or killed. Either way, sacrifices are always dead.

As we are crucified with Christ our flesh is sacrificed with His. But as Paul said, "Nevertheless I live; yet not I, but Christ liveth in me" (Gal. 2:20). As we present our bodies (flesh) as sacrifices (as we hate our own lives), our fleshy part of this new seed dies, and the life of Christ appears within us as evident by the presence of the fruit of the Spirit.

I referred to Mark 8:34 a few pages ago. Many have found this passage confusing: "Whosoever will come after me, let him deny himself, and take up his cross, and follow me." I know of several people who have carried large crosses over great distances as a "witness" for Christ. I suppose they were trying to promote the kingdom of God, but they may have been sending an inaccurate message. Jesus was not asking us to identify with Him as He carried the cross outside the city gate of Jerusalem; He wants us to identify with Him when He was nailed to it. *He does not want us to carry the cross; He wants us to die on it.* Carrying the cross can be bondage and a form of religion or works.

So many desire to follow Christ, but they are unable to do so and become frustrated. They try to live as He lived, then fail because they are doing these works or efforts out of their own abilities (their own souls). This life is the religious life. Religion is man's attempt to reach God through his own understanding, while the kingdom of God is God's calling of man to Himself in a relationship.

We are all guilty of this at times. We try to improve our souls through social advancement, education, and a good reputation with others. We try to satisfy our souls with delicacies, luxuries, and the pleasing of our senses (sensual). Many try to improve their souls by serving others—self-denial for the sake of later reward. These are all good, but from the good side of the wrong tree. These good things are actually darkness or evil, because they do not bring life. If we are to follow Jesus, we are to follow Him first in His death. It is only after we have followed Him in His death that we are able to follow Him in His life.

Just as the thief is free from stealing only after he is dead, we are free from sin only when we are dead. Jesus instructed, "If any man will come after me, let him deny himself, and take up his cross daily, and follow me" (Luke 9:23). Paul wrote, "I die daily" (1 Cor. 15:31). The only way we "get dead" is by denying our souls and hating our lives by rejecting our sinful flesh. This is not just rejecting the evil behavior, but our whole flesh—who we are in Adam—so we can begin to understand who we are in Christ.

The benefit of this appears in Romans 6:7: "For he that is dead is freed from sin." We experience escape from bondage as we die daily, as Paul did, to sin. For the believer who is growing the Seed and producing fruit, dying always brings life.

In Dying, Two Join

According to John 12:24, the seed, which is buried in the earth, remains by itself unless it dies, and this suggests that dying would join it to another. How can this be? Romans 6:4–7 says:

Therefore we are buried with him [Jesus] by
baptism into death: that like as Christ was raised
up from the dead by the glory of the Father, even
so we also should walk in newness of life. For if
we have been planted together in the likeness of
his death, we shall be also in the likeness of his
resurrection. Knowing this, that our old man is
crucified with him, that the body of sin might
be destroyed, that henceforth we should not
serve sin. For he that is dead is freed from sin.

Isn't this amazing? Verse 4 says we are buried with Jesus just as
the seed is buried, and verse 5 even goes further to say we are
"planted" together with Jesus. As we die to this world (hate
our own lives), we are planted, and baptism is our funeral.

If we desire to be like Jesus in His resurrection, we must
first be like Him in His death. Note the comparisons: We are
planted or buried with Jesus through baptism into death (the
seed falls into the ground and dies), and our old man is crucified with Jesus (the seed must die to be joined to another).
Then we shall be like Him in His resurrection and walk in
newness of life (a new plant begins to grow). We must understand that it is through death that we receive eternal life.

In verse 6 we see that the old man is crucified with Jesus,
for it is not enough just to die to enter the kingdom of God;
we must die or be crucified *with Jesus*. Many Eastern religions
as well as addiction treatments teach a self-death or yielding

to a "higher power." Dying alone will not give life. We must be buried with the "incorruptible seed" (Jesus) to receive life. To become the new man, we must receive the new Seed (Jesus) into our soil (hearts). We must receive this new life that is His life.

If we combine some of the truths God has been showing us, we can see the "great mystery" that Paul referred to in Ephesians. Just as the covenant of marriage begins when the two become one flesh, our covenant with Christ begins when we become one "flesh" with Him. The seed buried in the ground has two parts, and the fleshy part dies as the embryo gives life. These two parts are why we are buried or planted with Jesus. *There are two parts to this "seed," and they are our flesh and His Spirit.* Once buried (planted), our flesh has to die for His Spirit to give eternal life and this life becomes evident in us as we bear the fruit of the Spirit. Again, is this not amazing?

Soul Death Before Physical Death

We must understand that before Jesus Himself could give up His physical life, He first had to deny His soul. John 12:27 says, "Now is my soul troubled; and what shall I say? Father, save me from this hour: but for this cause came I unto this hour." Jesus was a "troubled soul" constantly tempted to disobey His Father, but He did only what His Father desired. The night before His physical death, the struggle with His soul was so strong in the Garden of Gethsemane that His sweat mixed with blood from the intense pressure and stress of the situation.

Jesus' soul did not want to go to the cross. "And he went a little farther, and fell on his face, and prayed, saying, O my Father, if it be possible, let this cup pass from me: nevertheless not as I will, but as thou wilt" (Matt. 26:39). It was in the Garden of Gethsemane that Jesus overcame the world and resisted the poison fruit of the tree of the knowledge of good and evil for the last time. The following day He hung on that tree of the knowledge of good and evil (cross) to take the curse away from us.

Jesus denied His soul and:

> for the joy that was set before him endured the cross, despising the shame, and is set down at the right hand of the throne of God. For consider him that endured such contradiction of sinners against himself, lest ye be wearied and faint in your minds [souls]. Ye have not yet resisted unto blood, striving against sin (Hebrews 12:2–4)

Notice it says we have not resisted unto blood as we have tried to avoid sin. This is not referring to the blood Jesus shed on the cross, for that was not a resistance to sin (He was already dead). His resistance to sin occurred the night before in the Garden of Gethsemane. Therefore, this blood Hebrews mentions is the blood He sweated that evening.

As a physician, I know it is possible that when someone is in extreme anguish, his red blood cells can mix with sweat and produce a red color that appears as blood. Let me be clear that Jesus' blood mixed with sweat was not an atonement for sin but merely a result of the pressure of resisting sin.

We must resist sin—hate our souls—and be willing to lose them in order to save them unto eternal life. We must lose our souls for Jesus' sake to be born again. As the seed must die before it can grow, we must be buried or planted with Jesus to walk in newness of life. We must be crucified with Him to be resurrected with Him. Our souls, and not our physical existences, are the enemy of God. It is our souls that incur God's wrath, and we must deny our souls to become a "living sacrifice." This is the will of God.

Those who die with the Lord Jesus (are crucified with Him) have denied their souls. To these He gave the authority to become the children of God (John 1:12). Just as the seed has to fall into the ground and die, otherwise it remains alone, our souls, as long as they lift themselves up and desire to seek glory for themselves, will remain lonely and separated from God. The seed must die or deny itself (more specifically, consume its flesh), and we must deny our flesh. We must acknowledge that our souls are evil, corrupt, and sinful. We must learn to hate our souls, and our sinful state that is an enemy to God. In denying this soul, we bury it in the ground, signifying its death. This burying, which is the planting of the tree of life, will bring forth much fruit (John 12:24).

In God's kingdom, everything seems turned on its head: to live, we must die; to save our souls we must deny them; to love God, we must hate our lives. In God's Word, paradox appears common, but only to our depraved minds, which have little natural understanding of God's ways. As we die, as we reject our own understanding (our self or will), God's Spirit enlightens us and we may then obey the first commandment. We may truly live, be fruitful, and multiply.

Chapter 12
Two in Covenant

We have seen how planting the Seed of the tree of life pictures the beginning of our relationship or covenant with Christ. Another picture we examined is the covenant (intimate relationship) of marriage in which Christ is our Husband. Again, the picture is the husband "planting" the seed in the wife just as the sower plants seed in the soil. Not only must the seed be planted, but the seed must die. More specifically, the "fleshy" part (endosperm) of the seed dies as the embryo produces a new plant. We know that Jesus' flesh was crucified like the endosperm while His blood possessed power unto a new life or new plant (resurrection).

Furthermore, we have seen that it is through death that we receive life. It is not through physical death that we obtain eternal life but through the denial of our souls (emotions, intellect, desires, and will)—rejection of our sinful selves. This is hard to hear. *The gospel is not just that Jesus died for us, but that we have to die with Him.* We must deny our souls.

How does the denial of our souls make us righteous before God? We know "the wages of sin is death" (Rom. 6:23), but how does Christ's death pay the penalty for my sin? We have addressed this partially from several perspectives, but it is the concept of covenant that draws all this to a clearer understanding.

What *Covenant* Means

In this chapter we will see that it is through covenant (relationship) with the Lord Jesus that we are justified before God. Hebrews 9:15–17 says:

> And for this cause [Jesus] is the mediator of the
> new testament [covenant], that by means of
> death, for the redemption of the transgressions
> that were under the first testament, they which
> are called might receive the promise of eternal
> inheritance. For where a testament is, there must
> also of necessity be the death of the testator. For a
> testament is of force after men are dead: otherwise
> it is of no strength at all while the testator liveth.

Jesus is the only Mediator or "go-between" in this new covenant or testament (1 Tim. 2:5). We saw earlier that the word *testament* is from Latin and refers to a covenant or type of contract. It is translated from the Greek word *diatheke*, which is a contract that is enforced only when the one who makes the contract is dead.

When a lawyer prepares a document that determines who will receive your possessions in the case of your death, it is called a last will and testament. Your last will is your final desire, and your testament is a contract to be fulfilled at the time of your death. Usually a contract would involve payment to another in exchange for services, goods, and property. A testament or *diatheke* is a contract that delivers money, goods, and property to another according to your last desire or will when you die.

Again, this contract is enforced only after we are dead. If I were to take my last will and testament to a judge and ask him to enforce it, he would look at me and laugh because I am still living. But if he were provided proof of my death, he would order that my wishes be executed according to the contract.

In the same way, the contract or testament that Jesus mediates between us and God is the New Testament or new *diatheke*, a contract enforceable only after our deaths. This is what Hebrews 9:17 means: "For a testament is . . . of no strength at all while the testator liveth." The word "testator" means the one who is making the covenant or contract.

This ties in to Mark 8:35, which we have examined in detail: "For whosoever will save his life shall lose it; but whosoever shall lose his life for my sake and the gospel's, the same shall save it." Again, the seed must die in order to bear fruit, and the one making the covenant must die in order for the covenant to be enforced.

In Exodus 20, when God gave the Ten Commandments at Mount Sinai, the Israelites understood that it was only through death that they could enter into a relationship and covenant with God. "And they said unto Moses, Speak thou with us, and we will hear: but let not God speak with us, lest we die" (Ex. 20:19). The people of Israel understood that entering into this close (covenant) relationship with God would require their lives. They did not want this because they would have had to die by rejecting their souls and their own understanding.

Jonathan and David

In our present-day culture, we really do not understand the seriousness of covenant. This is evident in the superficial behavior and shallow faith of many who call themselves Christians. Our Western or occidental minds are primarily focused on preserving the physical life. This is quite obvious in our vast spending on health care, and the strong bondage our culture has to Satan because of our terrifying fear of death.

The best example of a covenant relationship between two intimate friends is the one between Jonathan and David in 1 Samuel. Their relationship is a picture of the covenant between Jesus and us.

"And it came to pass, when he had made an end of speaking unto Saul, that the soul of Jonathan was knit with the soul of David, and Jonathan loved him as his own soul . . . Then Jonathan and David made a covenant" (1 Sam. 18:1,3). The

131

Scripture continues in a later chapter, "And Jonathan Saul's son arose, and went to David into the wood, and strengthened his hand in God . . . And they two made a covenant before the Lord: and David abode in the wood, and Jonathan went to his house" (1 Sam. 23:16,18). Notice that this was a covenant made between the king's son, who had everything, and a shepherd boy.

Jonathan denied his soul—denied his position and power as heir to the throne—when it came to David because he loved him so much. Jesus loved us so much that He denied His own soul to the point of death so that He could be in covenant with us. In the same way, 1 Samuel 18:3 says that Jonathan made this covenant with David because "he loved him as his own soul," and this is the same as loving your neighbor as yourself. This is an unconditional, unselfish love (Greek word: *agape*) that comes only from God.

Keeping the covenant was more important than keeping one's own life. David said to Jonathan, "Therefore thou shalt deal kindly with thy servant; for thou hast brought thy servant into a covenant of the LORD with thee: notwithstanding, if there be in me iniquity, slay [kill] me thyself " (1 Sam. 20:8). David asked Jonathan to kill him if he found any deceitfulness or evil in him, or if he did not honor the covenant.

The passage continues, "So Jonathan made a covenant with the house of David, saying, Let the LORD even require it at the hand of David's enemies. And Jonathan caused David to swear again, because he loved him: for he loved him as he loved his own soul" (vv. 16–17). Jonathan made this covenant with David before the Lord in that the Lord would "require it," meaning the Lord would make Jonathan obey the covenant or be killed by the enemies of David. Keeping the covenant was that vital.

Trading Clothes

"And Jonathan stripped himself of the robe that was upon him, and gave it to David, and his garments, even to his sword, and to his bow, and to his girdle [belt]" (1 Sam. 18:4). Jonathan gave his robe and other garments to David. Then David put on Jonathan's. Jonathan is a picture of Jesus, and David is a picture of us. Jesus is the Son of the King who has everything, and we are mere shepherd boys. Jesus has made this covenant with us because He loves us as His own soul. He gives us His clothes of righteousness, and we give him our filthy rags. Colossians 3:12–14 tells us to "put on" the Lord Jesus' righteousness just as we do clothing. In this new covenant we actually enrobe ourselves in the Lord Jesus.

This exchange of clothing occurs in marriage as well. Why do you think a bride wears white? "And to her was granted that she should be arrayed in fine linen, clean and white: for the fine linen is the righteousness of saints" (Rev. 19:8). The bride wearing white linen is a picture of Jesus giving us (His bride) His robes of righteousness. If we put on His righteousness, what does Jesus put on? He puts on our nakedness (Rev. 3:17). This is why He had to be naked on the cross. He had to wear what Adam wore at the time of the transgression (Gen. 3:7).

Swapping Weapons and Enemies

Next, we see that Jonathan gave David his sword, his bow, and his belt. The belt carried the weapons. As they exchanged belts, they were exchanging weapons. This represented trading enemies, in that the enemies of David now became Jonathan's and vice versa.

It is the same with Christ. When we make covenant with Him, our enemies become His.

> If it be possible, as much as lieth in you, live
> peaceably with all men. Dearly beloved, avenge
> not yourselves, but rather give place unto wrath:
> for it is written, Vengeance is mine; I will repay,
> saith the Lord. Therefore if thine enemy hunger,
> feed him; if he thirst, give him drink: for in so
> doing thou shalt heap coals of fire on his head.
> Be not overcome of evil, but overcome evil
> with good. (Romans 12:18–21)

We are to love our enemies and overcome them with good, and no longer should we fear or worry about what any men do to us. For they are God's enemies now, and it is God's responsibility to deal with them under this covenant. Therefore, we are set free to love those who hate us and persecute us. It is not us they are persecuting; it is Jesus.

In the same way, the enemies of Jesus become our enemies. Ephesians 6:12 says, "We wrestle not against flesh and blood, but against principalities, against powers, against the rulers of the darkness of this world, against spiritual wickedness in high places." Our enemy is not a man who hurts us, but the evil spirit that motivates him. We must understand the spiritual bondage of others and the deception they suffer. Why should we be angry with someone who has little option to act any other way?

Not only do we exchange enemies, but we exchange weapons. No longer do we continue in our weapons of anger, hatred, revenge, gossiping, murder, and all the lust of the flesh. Our new weapons are mercy, humility, patience, and love. "A soft answer turneth away wrath: but grievous words stir up anger" (Prov. 15:1).

When we are meek and lowly, we can calm the anger of the fiercest beast. There is such peace and power in these weapons. This is why Jesus said:

> Unto him that smiteth thee on the one cheek
> offer also the other; and him that taketh away
> thy cloke forbid not to take thy coat also. Give
> to every man that asketh of thee; and of him
> that taketh away thy goods ask them not again.

And as ye would that men should do to you,
do ye also to them likewise. For if ye love them
which love you, what thank have ye? For sinners
also love those that love them. And if ye do good
to them which do good to you, what thank have
ye? For sinners also do even the same . . . But
love ye your enemies and do good, and lend,
hoping for nothing again; and your reward
shall be great, and ye shall be the children of
the Highest: for he is kind unto the unthankful
and to the evil. (Luke 6:29–33,35)

The fruits of love (toward our enemies), mercy, and humility
are the most powerful weapons ever conceived.

Trading Names

In making a covenant, the participants would also exchange
names. Abram made covenant with God, more specifically
Elohiym. Abram took part of *Elohiym's* name and became
Abraham. Sarai then became Sarah. Up to this point in the
Scriptures, God was known simply as God. After this
covenant, He became the God of Abraham. Then came Isaac
and later Jacob, and God "became the God of Abraham,
Isaac, and Jacob." Throughout the rest of the Old Testament
this is His name. Sometimes it is shortened to "the God of
our fathers" or "the God of Israel."

We need to understand that when we make covenant with others we actually exchange places, in that they become us and we become them. This is how David became king of Israel. Yes, we know that Samuel anointed David, but how could David become king without a complete overthrow of the government and army?

David made covenant with Jonathan. They exchanged places, and David actually became Jonathan. First Samuel 23:17 says, "[Jonathan] said unto [David], Fear not: for the hand of Saul my father shall not find thee; and thou shalt be king over Israel, and I shall be next unto thee; and that also Saul my father knoweth." Jonathan understood when he made covenant with David that David would be the heir and be king over Israel as Saul's son in place of himself. Jonathan was son of the king, the heir to the throne and all the power was to be his, but he gave it all up for David because he loved David more than his own soul. This is denying one's soul.

Jesus' Amazing Trade with Us

In the same way, Jesus gave up being King and Priest, that we may become "kings and priests" (Rev. 1:6) we are not priests to each other but to a lost world that knows Him only superficially. Yet He still exists as our high priest forever (Heb. 7:17), making intercession for us before the Father. Even more than king and priest, the Lord Jesus was God, and He took on this weak, feeble flesh and suffered, because He loved us more than His own soul.

Let this mind be in you, which was also in
Christ Jesus: Who, being in the form of God,
thought it not robbery to be equal with God:
But made himself of no reputation, and took
upon him the form of a servant, and was made
in the likeness of men: And being found in fashion as a man, he humbled himself, and became
obedient unto death, even the death of the cross
(Philippians 2:5–8)

As Jonathan and David exchanged places in their
covenant, we exchange places with the Lord Jesus. As we deny
our souls because we love Him more than our souls, we enter
into this covenant with Him before God. At that time, *He
takes on our sinful flesh, and we receive His life-giving Spirit.* Is
not that amazing?

When Paul said, "I am crucified with Christ" (Gal. 2:20)
it was true, for that was not Jesus on the cross, that was Paul.
That was not Jesus on the cross, that was me. He became me
and suffered and died in my place. God therefore accepted
Jesus' death for the wages of my sin because of the covenant
Jesus made with me. I am now justified before God because
of the Lord Jesus. This is how our sin debt is paid, and furthermore this is how the body of sin (the sinner) is crucified
and set free from the bondage of the fear of death. This is the
New Testament or new covenant.

Paul went on in the same verse to say, "Nevertheless I live; yet not I, but Christ liveth in me and the life which I now live in the flesh I live by the faith of the Son of God, who loved me, and gave himself for me." As Jesus exchanged places with us and bore our sin and shame on that cross, we exchange places with Him and live in His righteousness and His kingdom through this new covenant. We must see ourselves as dead on that cross, which leaves only Christ alive to live in us. I must lose my soul to have Christ expressed in me through His Spirit, which grows and produces fruit.

We cannot see this picture on our own, but the Spirit of God must reveal it to us. God has to show us that we are dead. Through the experience of this revelation, we may "reckon" ourselves "dead to sin" but "alive unto God through Jesus Christ our Lord" (Rom. 6:11). *Growing in faith and understanding is simply to grow in our ability to see ourselves dead to sin and alive to Him.*

"Reckon" is an accounting term. It simply means *to count*. As I grow in faith (faith comes by hearing the Word of God), I am better able to count more of myself dead through the revelation of the Spirit. This is the beginning of the Christian life, and the new birth. The "fleshy" part of the seed must die just as the "testator" must die for the covenant to be in force. It is through this new covenant that we are justified before God. It is only through the Mediator of this covenant, the Lord Jesus, that we may have relationship with God unto life eternal.

In covenant with Jesus, we have traded sin for righteousness, our enemies for God's, our status as nobodies for Jesus' rank as priests. To maintain this covenant, we must not only rely upon His death on the cross, but fulfill the other part of the gospel: die *with* Jesus. As we do so, we begin to obey God's first commandment to mankind; we became fruitful and can multiply.

Conclusion
Jesus Our Example

Jesus is our sacrifice, and He is our example. He is the grain of wheat that fell to the ground and died. His death on the cross, and subsequent shedding of blood, made atonement for our sin. Praise God! But the night before He died He was our example in the Garden of Gethsemane. He denied His soul and said, "Nevertheless not my will, but thine, be done" (Luke 22:42). We must deny our cursed, self-promoting, self-preserving, self-motivated souls to enter the covenant and receive eternal life.

This new life is not a totally "free gift"; it costs us our souls. "He that loveth his life [soul] shall lose it; and he that hateth his life [soul] in this world shall keep it unto life eternal" (John 12:25). We must lose our souls to receive the eternal life of the eternal tree. It is only through this rejection of our souls that we can exchange places with Christ. Then God sees us on the cross, and He sees Jesus in us. Amen! We become sons of God, and God loves us just as much as He loves Jesus. Remember, we must follow His example and deny our souls to receive the blessing of Christ's sacrifice in this new covenant.

Jesus is also our example in suffering temptation and overcoming the one tempting, Satan. Look again at Hebrews 2:14–18:

> Forasmuch then as the children are partakers of
> flesh and blood, he also himself likewise took
> part of the same; that through death he might
> destroy him that had the power of death, that is,
> the devil; and deliver them who through fear of
> death were all their lifetime subject to bondage.
> For verily he took not on him the nature of
> angels; but he took on him the seed of Abraham.
> Wherefore in all things it behoved him to be
> made like unto his brethren, that he might be a
> merciful and faithful high priest in things per-
> taining to God, to make reconciliation for the
> sins of the people. For in that he himself hath
> suffered being tempted, he is able to succour
> them that are tempted.

This passage clearly states that Satan, the devil, has the power of death, and we are in bondage to Satan because of our fear of death. This bondage is present throughout our lifetimes, but if we lose our souls there is no fear of death.

Since we are "partakers of flesh and blood," Jesus also became flesh and blood. He did not take the nature of angels but took on the nature of the seed of Abraham (by becoming a man). This curse that came upon Adam for his disobedience, which resulted in all mankind eating from the tree of the knowledge of good and evil, could not be broken by an angel. Therefore, God took on the nature of the only one who could erase the curse. Specifically, God fulfilled the promise He made to Abraham by becoming a man, the Seed of Abraham, who is Christ Jesus. He became our High Priest in that He offered the sacrifice on our behalf, namely Himself, to reconcile us to God.

Hebrews 12:18 explains that Jesus suffered from being tempted as we do and is therefore able to provide help to us when we are tempted. The temptation, no matter how Satan presents it, always expresses itself as one of three types: lust of the flesh, lust of the eye, and the sinful pride of life. These three forms of temptation all are aimed at the desire to please or exalt our souls.

Jesus' death resulted in freeing us from the curse and reconciling us to God in a relationship (covenant). Once we are reconciled, we are set free from the curse and now have a choice in whether to please either our souls or God. Jesus is an example to us in how He denied His soul in the face of temptation (Garden of Gethsemane), and His grace provides us power to deny our souls as well (1 Cor. 10:13).

So many desire to be like Christ in His next appearance (in glory), and we may see this in the preaching of many as they demonstrate their "power" in volume and assurance

143

(arrogance). But we must unite in His suffering to unite in His resurrection, and we must first have His humility and gentleness. If God is to speak to us, we should expect "a still small voice" (1 Kings 19:12). Paul said, "My strength is made perfect in weakness" (2 Cor. 12:9). As Jesus denied His soul to serve the will of His Father, so shall we. "As he [Jesus] is, so are we" (1 John 4:17).

We must understand that denying our souls is denying our emotions, intellect, desires, and will. Think about it: the very best and most intelligent thought we ever had on our own is cursed and of Satan. It came from the soul we have to deny. The desires to please our flesh and be treated well are from our souls, which we must deny. This message is not frequently taught, and it may not fill the pews, but it is the truth. When we deny our souls, we cut the tree of the knowledge of good and evil growing in us off at the roots, and allow the tree of life (eternal life) to grow and bear the (eternal) fruit of the Spirit in us.

And again, what is this eternal life? John 17:2-3 says, "As thou hast given him [Jesus] power over all flesh, that he should give eternal life to as many as thou hast given him. And this is life eternal, that they might know [*ginosko*] thee the only true God, and Jesus Christ, whom thou hast sent." Eternal life is knowing the Father through the Son, Jesus Christ. It is the intimate relationship denoted by the Greek word *ginosko*. It is a covenant with your Creator through Jesus. It does not begin after your physical death but begins with the death or the denial of your soul. At this point you are born again, enter the kingdom of God, enter into eternal life, and are saved from the judgment to come. It is not through any religious act, but through a covenant (relationship) with the Lord Jesus.

God told Adam, Noah, Abraham, Jacob, and his descendants through Moses to "be fruitful and multiply," and God is still telling us today through His Son, the Lord Jesus. As we receive the spiritual seed from the spiritual tree, we can yield spiritual fruit or the fruit of the Spirit. This Seed, who is Jesus, can be planted in others, allowing us to multiply.

We have examined the process of the seed being planted, germinating, and dying, and how this is the picture of covenant, and our need to deny ourselves. This requires faith. The seed has to sacrifice the "fleshy" part in germinating so that the embryo can give life. In the same way, we have to sacrifice (crucify) our flesh for the Spirit of God to give us life—eternal life. Remember, Jesus dying on the cross does not save us or give us life. It is when we die (our souls) with Him that eternal life is germinated within us.

Again, this is the only way spiritual fruit grows, and the only way we fulfill God's first commandment, to "Be fruitful, and multiply."

BIBLIOGRAPHY

Concordances:

Strong, James. *The New Strong's Exhaustive Concordance of the Bible*. Nashville, TN: Thomas Nelson, 1996.

Wigram, George V., ed. *The Englishman's Hebrew Concordance of the New Testament*. Peabody, MA: Hendrickson, 1999.

————. *The Englishman's Hebrew Concordance of the Old Testament*. Peabody, MA: Hendrickson, 1999.

Interlinears:

Marshall, Alfred, trans. *Parallel New Testament in Greek and English*. Grand Rapids, MI: Zondervan, 1980.

Green, Jay P., trans. *The Interlinear Greek-English New Testament*. Grand Rapids, MI: Baker, 1996.

————. *The Interlinear Hebrew-English Old Testament*. Lafayette, IN: Sovereign Grace, 2000.

Lexicons:

Brown, Francis, S. Driver, and Charles Briggs. *The Brown-Driver-Briggs Hebrew and English Lexicon*. Peabody, MA: Hendrickson, 1999.

Vine, W. E. *Vine's Complete Expository Dictionary of Old and New Testament Words*. Nashville, TN: Thomas Nelson, 1996.

Zodhiates, Spiros, ed. *The Complete Word Study Dictionary New Testament*. Chattanooga, TN: AMG International, 1993.